SO-ANG-391

VOYAGES
RESEARCH-BASED MATHEMATICS

EXCURSIONS

Developed by
Metropolitan Teaching and Learning Company
and
The School District of Hillsborough County

SENIOR AUTHORS
AL SORIANO, JACK BEERS

Senior Authors
ALBERT SORIANO, JR.
Former Supervisor, Elementary Mathematics
School District of Hillsborough County

JACK BEERS
Vice President, Math and Science
Metropolitan Teaching and
Learning Company

Author, K–5; Program Manager, K–2
JANET WHITE
Elementary Mathematics
School District of Hillsborough County

Author, K–5; Program Manager, 3–5
JOHN FAHLE
Elementary Mathematics
School District of Hillsborough County

Author, K–5; Technical Design Manager, K–5
KEITH ABORN
Elementary Mathematics
School District of Hillsborough County

Author, K–5; Lead Kindergarten Consultant
BARBARA KNOX
Elementary Mathematics
School District of Hillsborough County

Author, School District of Hillsborough County
SCOTT WEAVER

Contributing Authors/Editors, School District of Hillsborough County
JEFFREY GUERRA
JOHN PERRY
DAVID WHITMAN

Contributing Resource Teachers, Elementary Mathematics, School District of Hillsborough County
RITA DUGAN
ELIZABETH GLENN (retired)

School District of Hillsborough County

School Board Members
GLENN BARRINGTON
CAROLYN BRICKLEMYER
JENNIFER FALIERO
CAROL W. KURDELL

JACK R. LAMB, ED.D.
CANDY OLSON
DORIS ROSS REDDICK

Superintendent
EARL LENNARD, PH.D.

Deputy Superintendent for Instruction
BETH SHIELDS

Deputy Superintendent for Instructional Support
JIM HAMILTON, PH.D.

Assistant Superintendent, Business and Information Technology Services
MICHAEL BOOKMAN, PH.D.

Assistant Superintendent for Instruction
MICHAEL GREGO, PH.D.

General Director of Elementary Education
JOYCE G. HAINES, PH.D.

Supervisor, Elementary Mathematics
LIA CRAWFORD

Design: Debrah Welling
Cover: Charles Yuen

© 2003, 2004 School District of Hillsborough County.
Published by Metropolitan Teaching and Learning Company, a division of Cambium Learning, Inc. Printed in the United States of America.

All rights reserved. No part of this work may be reproduced, transmitted, or utilized in any form or by any means, electronic, mechanical, or otherwise, including photocopying and recording, or by any storage and retrieval system, without prior written permission from Metropolitan Teaching and Learning Company.

Metropolitan Teaching and Learning Company
New York, New York

ISBN 1-58830-612-7

4 5 6 DBH 06

Table of Contents

TOPIC 3:
Geometry

TOPIC 4:
Whole Numbers and Decimals II

TOPIC 5:
Measurement

TOPIC 6:
Fractions

TOPIC 7:
Probability

TOPIC 1
Data Collection and Analysis

© School District of Hillsborough County. Copying this page without written permission of Metropolitan Teaching and Learning Company is illegal.

Name _____

What's My Favorite?

WHICH ONE?

Title: _____

Choices	Number (Tally)

HOME CONNECTION: HOME FAVORITE

Dear Parent or Guardian:

Your child has been learning how to take a survey. For the survey below, your child needs to decide on a topic, such as three favorite family foods or three favorite books. Please read the directions with your child. Encourage him or her to share with you how to take a survey. Have him or her share the survey's results with you before returning it to school.

➡ **Choose a topic for a survey of your family members. Fill in the title and draw or write three choices in the left-hand column. Write the tally in the right-hand column.**

Title: _____

Favorite _____	Number (Tally)

My family's favorite _____ is _____.

© School District of Hillsborough County. Copying this page without written permission of Metropolitan Teaching and Learning Company is illegal.

Name _____

Button, Button, Who Has the Button?

SHOW IT!

Title: _____

GRAPH IT!

Title: _____

(blank graph grid: 3 columns by 7 rows, with three shaded boxes below the columns)

Key: 1 _____ stands for 1 cracker.

Name _____

HOME CONNECTION: FAMILY SIZE

Dear Parent or Guardian:

Your child has been learning all about pictographs and how to make them. He or she has learned how to take information from a tally chart and show it on a pictograph. Talk with your child about the tally chart on the back of this sheet. Then he or she should create a pictograph to show the same information. Have you child share his or her pictograph with you when it is complete.

© School District of Hillsborough County. Copying this page without written permission of Metropolitan Teaching and Learning Company is illegal.

HOME CONNECTION: FAMILY SIZE

Carlos made a tally chart of the number of people each child in his class has in his or her family.

Family Size

Number of People	Number of Families
2	IIII
3	IIII III
4	IIII IIII
5 or more	III

➡ **Show the information in the tally chart in a pictograph.**

Title _____

2 people								
3 people								
4 people								
5 or more people								

© School District of Hillsborough County. Copying this page without written permission of Metropolitan Teaching and Learning Company is illegal.

Name _____

Block Out

LET'S EAT LUNCH!

pizza

hot dog

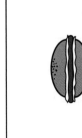

hamburger

Our Class's Favorite Lunch Choice

	1	2	3	4	5	6	7	8	9	10	11	12	13	14
hamburger														
hot dog														
pizza														

MY SHAPE GRAPH

➡ Count your pattern blocks and write how many you have of each. Then fill in the block graph.

10						
9						
8						
7						
6						
5						
4						
3						
2						
1						

TOPIC 1 Block Out

Name _____

HOME CONNECTION: SPORTS STAR

Dear Parent or Guardian:

Your child has been learning all about block graphs and how to make them. He or she has learned how to take information from a tally chart and show it on a block graph. Talk with your child about the tally chart on the back of this sheet. Then he or she should create a block graph to show the same information. Have your child share his or her block graph with you when it is complete.

© School District of Hillsborough County. Copying this page without written permission of Metropolitan Teaching and Learning Company is illegal.

HOME CONNECTION: SPORTS STAR

Lydia made a tally chart of the favorite summer sport of each child in her class.

Our Favorite Summer Sports

Favorite Sport	Number of People
Swimming	ЍЍ II
Basketball	III
Baseball	ЍЍ III
Soccer	ЍЍ II

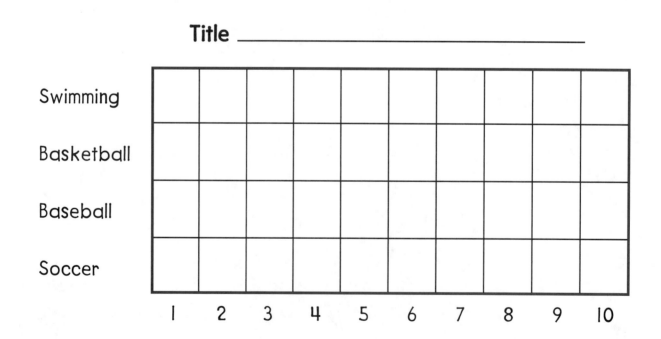

Title _____

TOPIC 2

Whole Numbers and Decimals I

© School District of Hillsborough County. Copying this page without written permission of Metropolitan Teaching and Learning Company is illegal.

Name _____

Numbers . . . Take Your Places!

ORDER UP! ORDER DOWN!

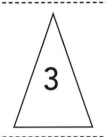 3
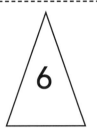 6
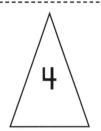 4
 2
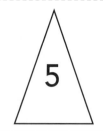 5

 7
11
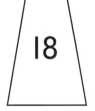 9
10
8

17
 16
 18
 15
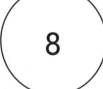 19

23
 20
 24
 21
 22

 39
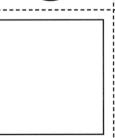 38
 40
 36
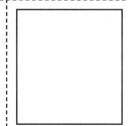 37

Name _____

© School District of Hillsborough County. Copying this page without written permission of Metropolitan Teaching and Learning Company is illegal.

WHAT'S MISSING?

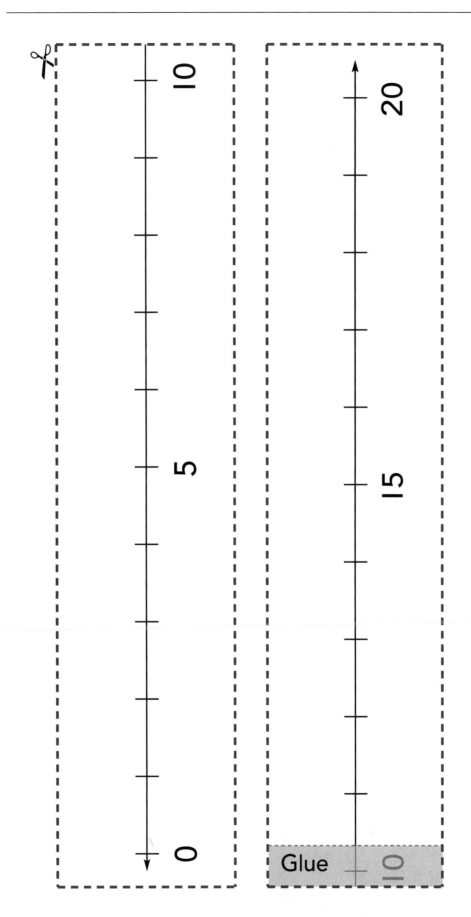

SYDNEY'S NUMBER WOES

➡ Sydney is responsible for returning books to the correct shelves in the library. Help Sydney. Cut out the books at the bottom of the page and glue them to the correct shelf.

from 0 to 10	from 11 to 20
from 21 to 30	from 31 to 40
from 41 to 50	from 51 to 60

13   19   7   49   22   39   34   2   57

© School District of Hillsborough County. Copying this page without written permission of Metropolitan Teaching and Learning Company is illegal.

WALK THIS WAY

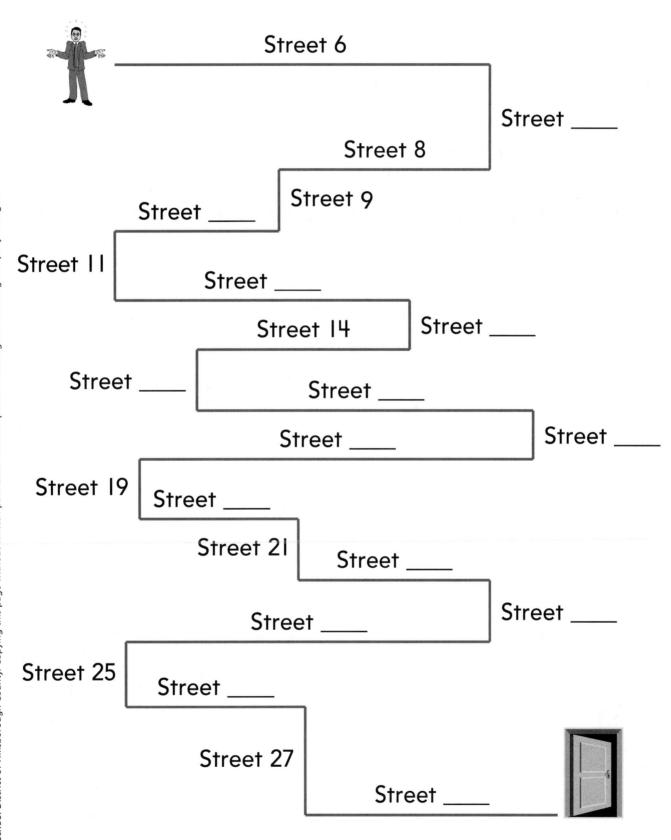

Street 6

Street ____

Street 8

Street 9

Street ____

Street 11

Street ____

Street 14

Street ____

Street ____

Street ____

Street ____

Street ____

Street 19

Street ____

Street 21

Street ____

Street ____

Street ____

Street 25

Street ____

Street 27

Street ____

© School District of Hillsborough County. Copying this page without written permission of Metropolitan Teaching and Learning Company is illegal.

HOME CONNECTION: ORDER! ORDER!

Dear Parent or Guardian:

Your child has been learning about the order of numbers. This is a card game for your child to play with one other person. Your child should record the results on separate pages. He or she should bring the record to class for sharing.

➡ **1.** Remove the kings, queens, jacks, and jokers from a deck of cards before playing. Place the remaining cards facedown in a pile.

➡ **2.** Take turns drawing three cards at a time from the deck. If two of the same number are drawn, return one to the deck and draw again.

➡ **3.** Read the numbers on the cards and place them in numerical order. Use the number line below for reference if needed.

➡ **4.** If the order is correct, write the numbers in order on a piece of paper and keep the cards. Play until all cards have been used. The player with the most cards wins.

➡ **5.** Repeat the game, using four cards and then five cards.

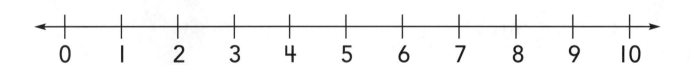

Name _____

Stairway to Math

STEP ON UP!

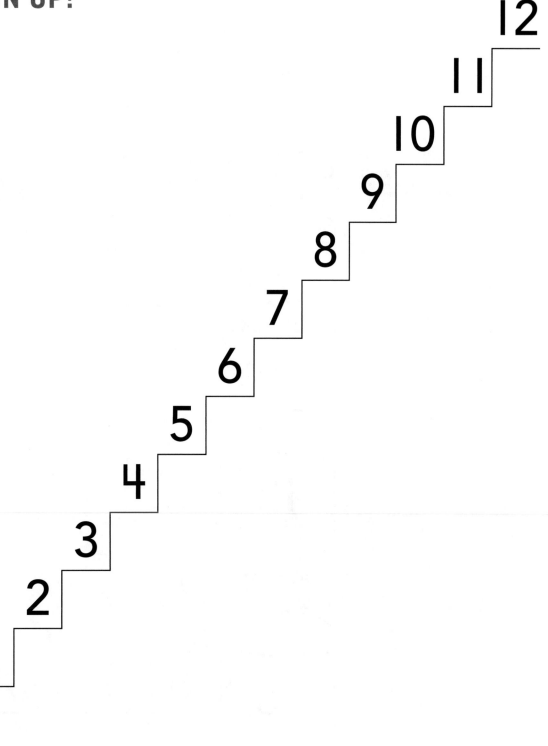

© School District of Hillsborough County. Copying this page without written permission of Metropolitan Teaching and Learning Company is illegal.

COUNTING ON

7

Count on 2

___ ___

8

Count on 3

___ ___ ___

12

Count on 1

___

16

Count on 3

___ ___ ___

TOPIC 2 Stairway to Math

10	20	30	40	50	60	70	80	90	100
5									
4									
3									
2									
1									

GETTING TO ONE HUNDRED

© School District of Hillsborough County. Copying this page without written permission of Metropolitan Teaching and Learning Company is illegal.

TOPIC 2 Stairway to Math

PICK A CARD

Dear Parent or Guardian:

Your child is learning to count on. For Pick a Card your child needs a deck of cards with the kings, queens, and jacks removed. Aces count as 1. Read the following directions and look at the example with your child. Support your child while he or she works through the chart. Ask him or her to share his or her results with you before bringing them back to school.

➡ **Draw one card from a deck. Write that number in the first column. (In the example, an 8 was drawn.) Count on 3 more. Record each number as you count. Then write the number you end on. Continue by drawing a new card to begin each row until you've filled in the whole chart.**

Start with	Count on 3			End on
8	9	10	11	11

Amazing Addition

COUNT THE BUTTONS

© School District of Hillsborough County. Copying this page without written permission of Metropolitan Teaching and Learning Company is illegal.

© School District of Hillsborough County. Copying this page without written permission of Metropolitan Teaching and Learning Company is illegal.

Name _____

MY FIRST BUTTON RECORD

red	yellow	total	red	yellow	total
___ +	___ =	___	___ +	___ =	___

red	yellow	total	red	yellow	total
___ +	___ =	___	___ +	___ =	___

red	yellow	total	red	yellow	total
___ +	___ =	___	___ +	___ =	___

red	yellow	total	red	yellow	total
___ +	___ =	___	___ +	___ =	___

red	yellow	total	red	yellow	total
___ +	___ =	___	___ +	___ =	___

red	yellow	total	red	yellow	total
___ +	___ =	___	___ +	___ =	___

red	yellow	total	red	yellow	total
___ +	___ =	___	___ +	___ =	___

red	yellow	total	red	yellow	total
___ +	___ =	___	___ +	___ =	___

red	yellow	total	red	yellow	total
___ +	___ =	___	___ +	___ =	___

red	yellow	total	red	yellow	total
___ +	___ =	___	___ +	___ =	___

MY SECOND BUTTON RECORD

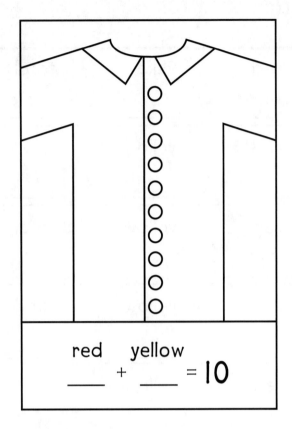

red   yellow

___ + ___ = 10

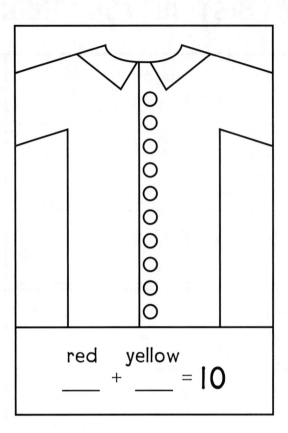

red   yellow

___ + ___ = 10

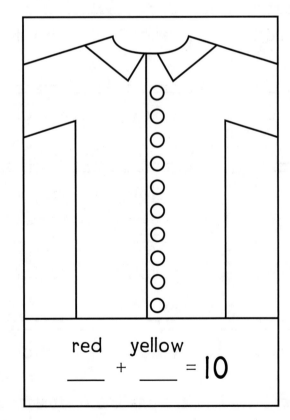

red   yellow

___ + ___ = 10

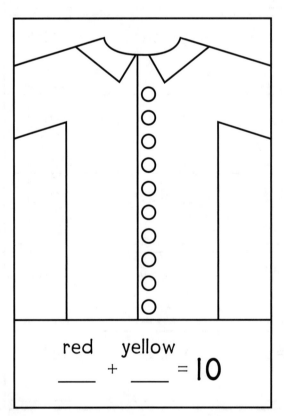

red   yellow

___ + ___ = 10

Name _____

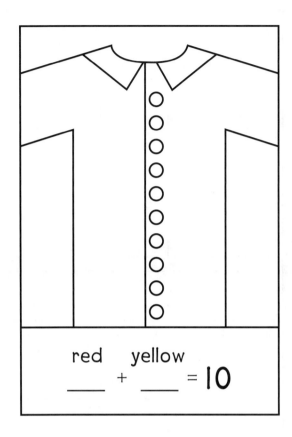

red   yellow
___ + ___ = 10

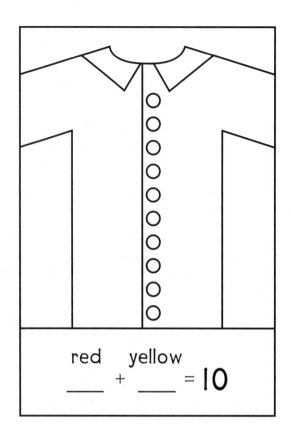

red   yellow
___ + ___ = 10

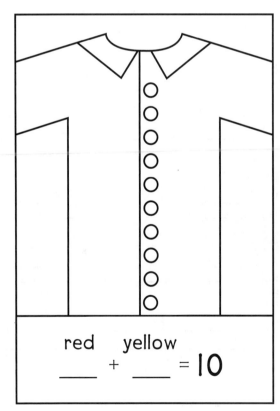

red   yellow
___ + ___ = 10

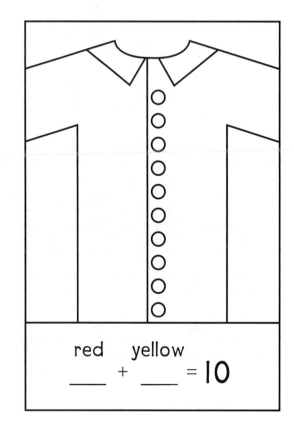

red   yellow
___ + ___ = 10

© School District of Hillsborough County. Copying this page without written permission of Metropolitan Teaching and Learning Company is illegal.

RECORDING SHEET FOR THE DOT GAME

_____ + _____ = _____   _____ + _____ = _____

_____ + _____ = _____   _____ + _____ = _____

_____ + _____ = _____   _____ + _____ = _____

_____ + _____ = _____   _____ + _____ = _____

_____ + _____ = _____   _____ + _____ = _____

_____ + _____ = _____   _____ + _____ = _____

_____ + _____ = _____   _____ + _____ = _____

_____ + _____ = _____   _____ + _____ = _____

_____ + _____ = _____   _____ + _____ = _____

_____ + _____ = _____   _____ + _____ = _____

_____ + _____ = _____   _____ + _____ = _____

TOPIC 2 Amazing Addition

Name _____

THE DOT GAME

© School District of Hillsborough County. Copying this page without written permission of Metropolitan Teaching and Learning Company is illegal.

Name _____

NUMBER CARDS FOR THE DOT GAME

0	1	2	3
4	5	6	7
8	9	10	11
12	13	14	15
16	17	18	

© School District of Hillsborough County. Copying this page without written permission of Metropolitan Teaching and Learning Company is illegal.

Name _____

HOME CONNECTION: ADDING DOTS

Dear Parent or Guardian:

Your child has been learning all about finding sums to 18. He or she has learned many strategies for finding these sums. Help him or her cut out the dot cards on the back of this sheet. Place the dot cards face down on a flat surface. Player 1 draws two dot cards. If he or she can add them successfully, he or she gets to keep the cards. If he or she cannot add them successfully, the cards are put back. Then Player 2 takes a turn. Continue playing until all cards have been won.

© School District of Hillsborough County. Copying this page without written permission of Metropolitan Teaching and Learning Company is illegal.

HOME CONNECTION: ADDING DOTS

TOPIC 2 Amazing Addition

© School District of Hillsborough County. Copying this page without written permission of Metropolitan Teaching and Learning Company is illegal.

Name _____

Which Way Should I Solve?

GOING SHOPPING!

| Race Car 10 pennies | Stuffed Rabbit 7 pennies | Sailboat 6 pennies | Train 9 pennies |

1. Act it Out.

I bought _____ and _____.

_____ + _____ = _____

2. Model it.

I bought _____ and _____.

_____ + _____ = _____

3. Draw it.

I bought _____ and _____.

_____ + _____ = _____

THE STRATEGY GAME

1. Circle the strategy card you picked.

Act It Out   Draw a Picture   Use Counters

Roll the dice and solve.

Write your number sentence: _____ + _____ = _____

2. Circle the strategy card you picked.

Act It Out   Draw a Picture   Use Counters

Roll the dice and solve.

Write your number sentence: _____ + _____ = _____

© School District of Hillsborough County. Copying this page without written permission of Metropolitan Teaching and Learning Company is illegal.

Name _____

THE STRATEGY GAME CARDS

Act It Out

Act It Out

Draw a Picture

Draw a Picture

Use Counters

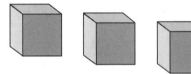

Use Counters

Pick Your Own Strategy

Pick Your Own Strategy

© School District of Hillsborough County. Copying this page without written permission of Metropolitan Teaching and Learning Company is illegal.

Name _____

HOME CONNECTION: SHOPPING LIST

Dear Parent or Guardian:

Your child has been learning different strategies for adding two numbers. Work with your child to make up 3 simple shopping lists that include multiple quantities of two items—for example, 4 apples and 2 bananas. Help your child write the 3 shopping lists on the back of this sheet. Then have your child act out, make drawings, or use models to find the total number of items. Have him or her complete the number sentences.

HOME CONNECTION: SHOPPING LIST

Shopping List 1

_____ + _____ = _____

Shopping List 2

_____ + _____ = _____

Shopping List 3

_____ + _____ = _____

TOPIC 2 **Which Way Should I Solve?**

Double Up

DOUBLES

➡ Write an addition sentence to match each double. The first one is done for you.

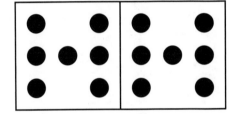

$$5 + 5 = 10$$

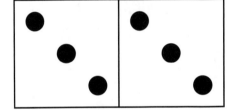

$$\underline{\quad} + \underline{\quad} = \underline{\quad}$$

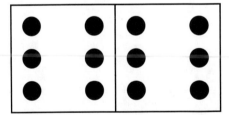

$$\underline{\quad} + \underline{\quad} = \underline{\quad}$$

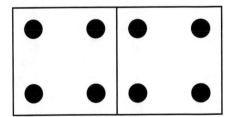

$$\underline{\quad} + \underline{\quad} = \underline{\quad}$$

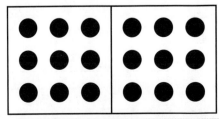

$$\underline{\quad} + \underline{\quad} = \underline{\quad}$$

$$\underline{\quad} + \underline{\quad} = \underline{\quad}$$

© School District of Hillsborough County. Copying this page without written permission of Metropolitan Teaching and Learning Company is illegal.

DOUBLES PLUS ONE

➡ Trace the gray dot to make a double plus one.
   Then trace the number sentences and write the sum.

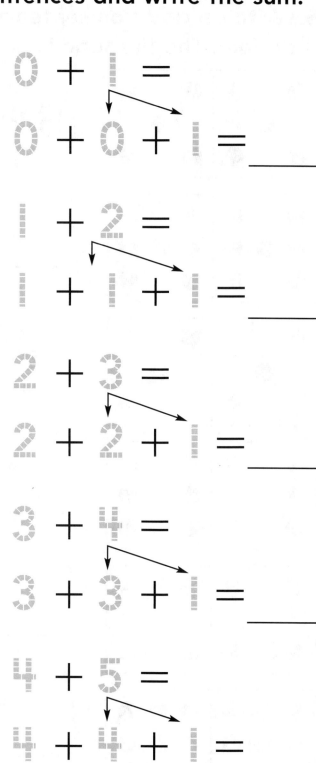

$$0 + 1 =$$
$$0 + 0 + 1 = \underline{\quad}$$

$$1 + 2 =$$
$$1 + 1 + 1 = \underline{\quad}$$

$$2 + 3 =$$
$$2 + 2 + 1 = \underline{\quad}$$

$$3 + 4 =$$
$$3 + 3 + 1 = \underline{\quad}$$

$$4 + 5 =$$
$$4 + 4 + 1 = \underline{\quad}$$

TOPIC 2 Double Up

Name _____

$$5 + 6 =$$

$$5 + 5 + 1 = \underline{\quad}$$

$$6 + 7 =$$

$$6 + 6 + 1 = \underline{\quad}$$

$$7 + 8 =$$

$$7 + 7 + 1 = \underline{\quad}$$

$$8 + 9 =$$

$$8 + 8 + 1 = \underline{\quad}$$

$$9 + 10 =$$

$$9 + 9 + 1 = \underline{\quad}$$

© School District of Hillsborough County. Copying this page without written permission of Metropolitan Teaching and Learning Company is illegal.

TOPIC 2 Double Up

Name _____

ROLLING DOUBLES

Draw your roll.	Circle.	Write the addition sentence.
☐ ☐	Doubles / Doubles + 1	| + | + | = || = |
☐ ☐	Doubles / Doubles + 1	| + | + | = || = |
☐ ☐	Doubles / Doubles + 1	| + | + | = || = |
☐ ☐	Doubles / Doubles + 1	| + | + | = || = |
☐ ☐	Doubles / Doubles + 1	| + | + | = || = |

TOPIC 2 Double Up

© School District of Hillsborough County. Copying this page without written permission of Metropolitan Teaching and Learning Company is illegal.

Name _____

HOME CONNECTION: SEEING STARS

Dear Parent or Guardian:

Your child has been learning all about doubles and doubles plus one. Help him or her cut out the star cards on the back of this sheet. Place the star cards face down on a flat surface. Player 1 draws two star cards. If the cards show a double or a double plus 1 and the player can add them successfully, he or she gets to keep the cards. If the cards are not a double or a double plus one or if the player cannot add them successfully, the cards are put back. Then Player 2 takes a turn. Continue playing until no more matches can be made.

HOME CONNECTION: SEEING STARS

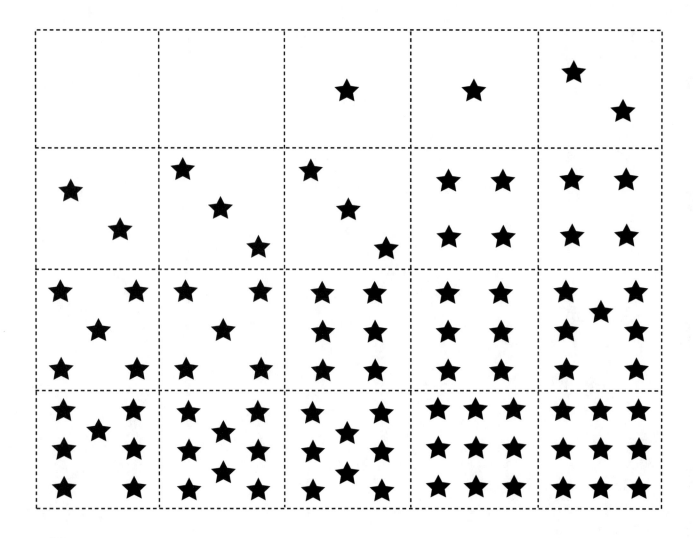

TOPIC 2 Double Up

© School District of Hillsborough County. Copying this page without written permission of Metropolitan Teaching and Learning Company is illegal.

Off We Go!

HOW MANY?

➡ **Ring as many groups of 10 stick children as you can. Then fill in the chart below.**

Number of FULL ten-rings	Number of children not in a FULL ten-ring

= _____ total children

FILL THE RINGS

➡ Draw 21 stick children in the rings below.
How many ten-rings could you fill?
Fill in the chart below.

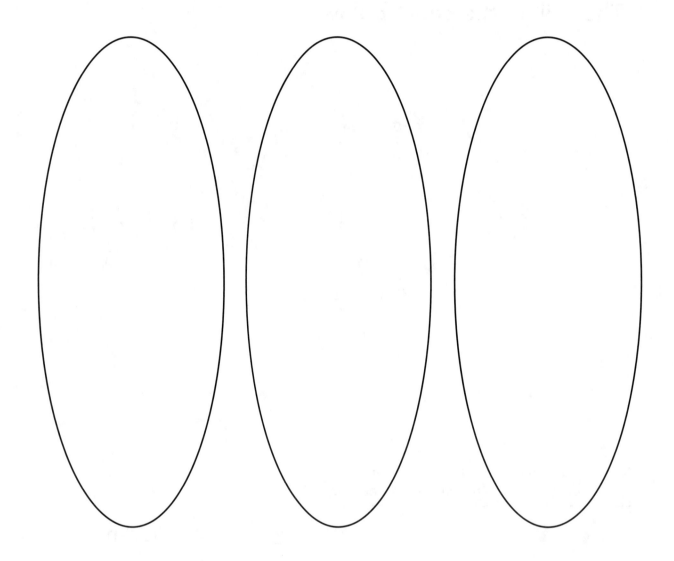

Number of FULL ten-rings	Number of children not in a FULL ten-ring

= ____ total children

Name _____

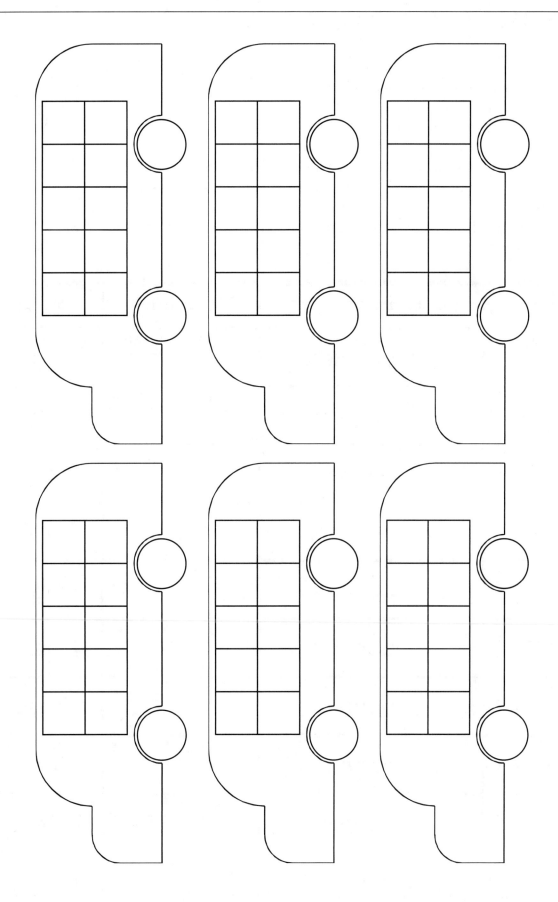

GET ON THE BUS!

© School District of Hillsborough County. Copying this page without written permission of Metropolitan Teaching and Learning Company is illegal.

HOME CONNECTION: TRADING

Dear Parent or Guardian:

Give your child a few pennies each day (vary the amounts) and have your child group and count the coins. When your child has ten or more pennies, he or she must trade ten pennies for a dime. Have your child daily record the following in the chart below:

1. the number of pennies he or she was given that day

2. the number of dimes and pennies he or she has altogether

3. the total value of his or her money

Continue this activity for ten days. Children should bring their chart into school at the end of the ten days.

	Today I was given:	I now have:		My Total:
		Dimes	Pennies	
Day 1	_____ pennies			Total:_____ ¢
Day 2	_____ pennies			Total:_____ ¢
Day 3	_____ pennies			Total:_____ ¢
Day 4	_____ pennies			Total:_____ ¢
Day 5	_____ pennies			Total:_____ ¢
Day 6	_____ pennies			Total:_____ ¢
Day 7	_____ pennies			Total:_____ ¢
Day 8	_____ pennies			Total:_____ ¢
Day 9	_____ pennies			Total:_____ ¢
Day 10	_____ pennies			Total:_____ ¢

Name _____

Is It Really 36?

WHAT'S IN THE BAG?

	tens	ones	Total Cubes
Bag A			
Bag B			
Bag C			
Bag D			

© School District of Hillsborough County. Copying this page without written permission of Metropolitan Teaching and Learning Company is illegal.

HOME CONNECTION: COUNTING AROUND THE HOME

Dear Parent or Guardian:

Your child has been learning how groups of more than ten objects can be organized into groups of ten and written as numerals on a place-value chart and as a total. Here is an example of what your child has been doing. You can reinforce your child's learning by helping him or her fill in the table below. First count out between 10 and 30 pieces of macaroni. Your child should then form as many groups of ten as possible. Then he or she can draw a simple picture of what the groups look like and complete the table.

	tens	ones	Total Cubes
	3	6	36

	tens	ones	Total Cubes

Panes!

NUMBER SHOW

➡ Cut apart the twelve boxes below.
   Make four sets of cards. Each set should
   contain one base-ten blocks card, one tens
   and ones card, and one numeral card.

© School District of Hillsborough County. Copying this page without written permission of Metropolitan Teaching and Learning Company is illegal.

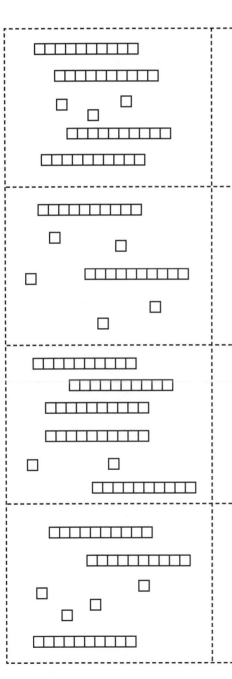

52	tens / ones 2 / 5
43	tens / ones 3 / 4
34	tens / ones 5 / 2
25	tens / ones 4 / 3

Name _____

GET TOGETHER

➡ **Glue matching cards in the same row.**

Base-ten blocks	Tens and ones	Numeral

Base-ten blocks	Tens and ones	Numeral

Base-ten blocks	Tens and ones	Numeral

Base-ten blocks	Tens and ones	Numeral

© School District of Hillsborough County. Copying this page without written permission of Metropolitan Teaching and Learning Company is illegal.

PANEVILLE

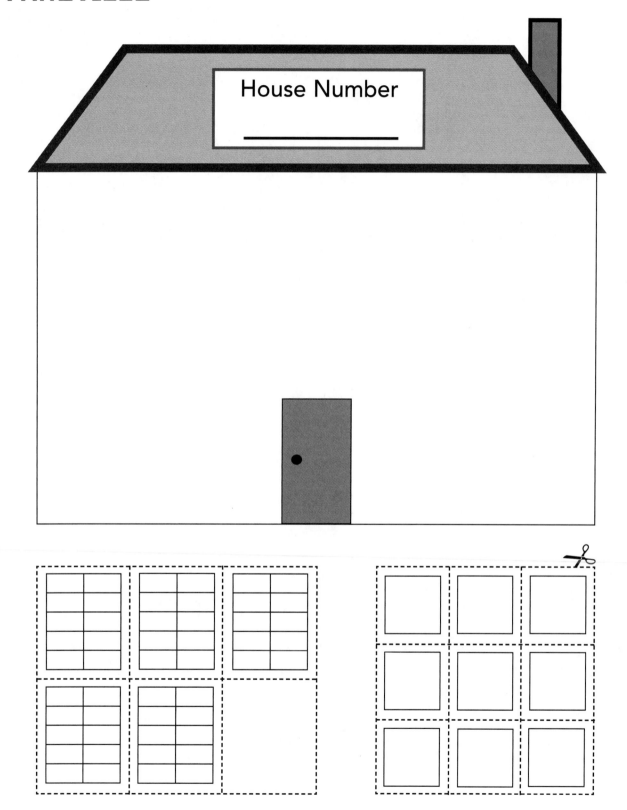

House Number

_____

© School District of Hillsborough County. Copying this page without written permission of Metropolitan Teaching and Learning Company is illegal.

Name _____

HOME CONNECTION: TOY STORE

Dear Parent or Guardian:

Your child has been learning about the tens and ones in two digit numbers. For example, your child now knows that in the number 54, there are 5 tens and 4 ones. Your child has learned that this number can be represented using tens and ones blocks. Have your child cut out the 10 pane windows and the 1 pane windows on the other side of this sheet. Have them decide how many of each they wish to use to complete the toy store. Then have them write the number they are showing with windows at the top of the store.

© School District of Hillsborough County. Copying this page without written permission of Metropolitan Teaching and Learning Company is illegal.

HOME CONNECTION: TOY STORE

Toy Store Number _____

TOPIC 3
Geometry

Name _____

Shape Off

SHAPES TO CUT OUT

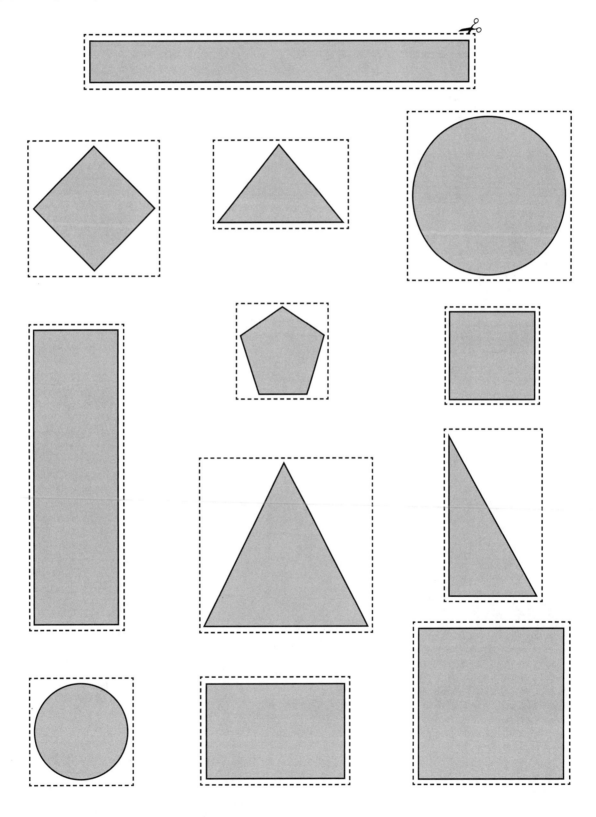

© School District of Hillsborough County. Copying this page without written permission of Metropolitan Teaching and Learning Company is illegal.

© School District of Hillsborough County. Copying this page without written permission of Metropolitan Teaching and Learning Company is illegal.

SHAPE SORT

Circle	Triangle
Rectangle	

SHAPE BEANBAG TOSS

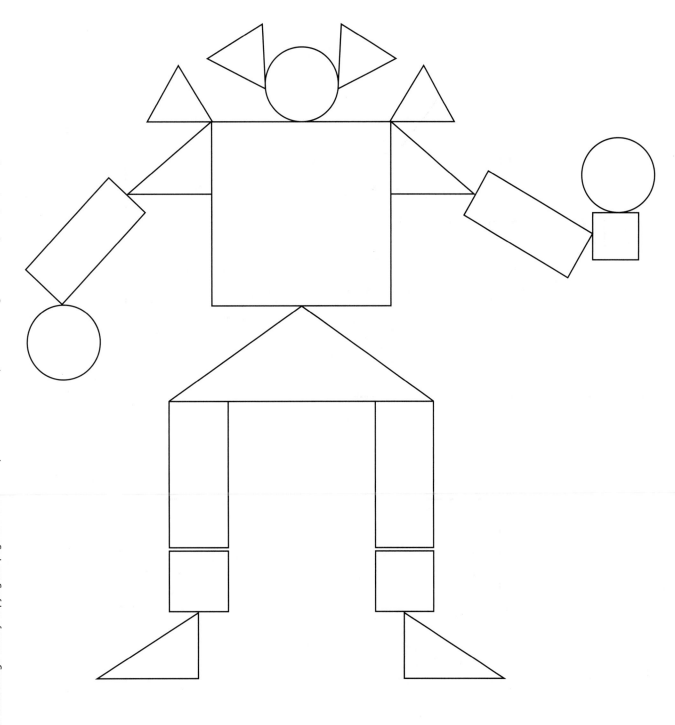

© School District of Hillsborough County. Copying this page without written permission of Metropolitan Teaching and Learning Company is illegal.

SHAPE SEARCH

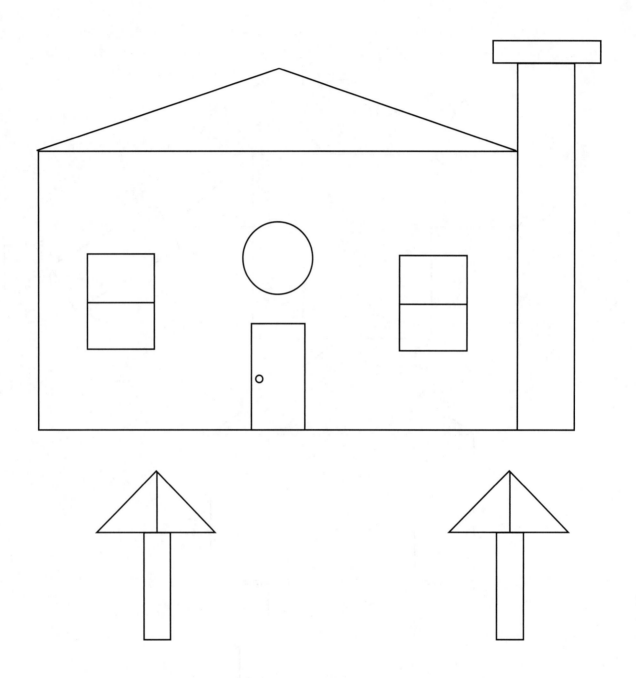

_____ circles _____ triangles _____ rectangles

TOPIC 3 Shape Off

HOME CONNECTION: SHAPES AT HOME

Dear Parent or Guardian:

Your child has been learning about shapes. Have your child point out different shapes he or she sees around the house. Have your child go on a shape hunt. Then, on the other side of this sheet, have him or her record what was found.

© School District of Hillsborough County. Copying this page without written permission of Metropolitan Teaching and Learning Company is illegal.

HOME CONNECTION: SHAPES AT HOME

TOPIC 3 Shape Off

© School District of Hillsborough County. Copying this page without written permission of Metropolitan Teaching and Learning Company is illegal.

Name _____

Making Pictures

SHAPES, SHAPES, EVERYWHERE

This shape is a _____.

It has _____ equal sides.

It has _____ vertices.

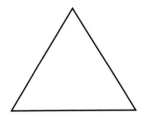

This shape is a _____.

It has _____ sides.

It has _____ vertices.

This shape is a _____.

It has _____ sides.

It has _____ vertices.

This shape is a _____.

It has _____ sides.

It has _____ vertices.

This shape is a _____.

It has _____ sides.

It has _____ vertices.

This shape is a _____.

It has _____ equal sides.

It has _____ vertices.

© School District of Hillsborough County. Copying this page without written permission of Metropolitan Teaching and Learning Company is illegal.

Name _____

PICTURE, PICTURE, WHERE IS THE PICTURE?

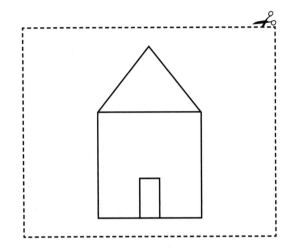

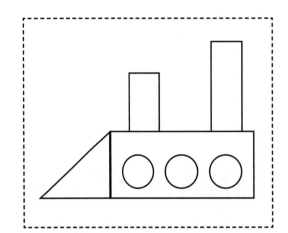

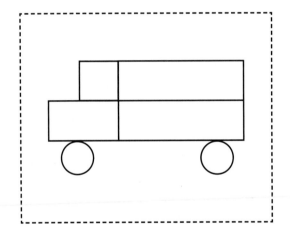

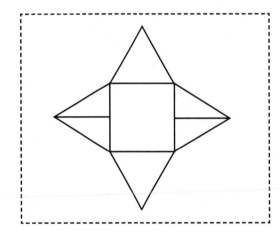

Color the circles red.

Color the squares blue.

Color the triangles yellow.

Color the rectangles green.

Name _____

My picture is made out of
one square.

Inside the square is a rectangle.

On top of the square is a triangle.

Which picture am I?

My picture is made from
rectangles.

I have one square, too.

I also have circles in my picture.

My picture has a square.

Outside the square there are
8 triangles.

My picture has 3 circles.

It also has 3 rectangles.

The left part of my picture is
a triangle.

© School District of Hillsborough County. Copying this page without written permission of Metropolitan Teaching and Learning Company is illegal.

BUILD A PICTURE!

In my picture, I used the following shapes:

Shape	Tally	Number of Shapes
square ☐		
rectangle ▭		
triangle △		
circle ○		
rhombus ◇		
other _____		

My partner used the following shapes:

Shape	Tally	Number of Shapes
square ☐		
rectangle ▭		
triangle △		
circle ○		
rhombus ◇		
other _____		

Name _____

HOME CONNECTION: SORTING SHAPES

Dear Parent or Guardian:

Your child has been learning how many sides and corners different shapes have. Read the instructions on the next page aloud to your child. Then have your child complete the page. Have your child share the finished page with you.

© School District of Hillsborough County. Copying this page without written permission of Metropolitan Teaching and Learning Company is illegal.

Color the circles red.

Color the squares blue.

Color the triangles yellow.

Color the other rectangles green.

I Spy Shapes

CLOWNING AROUND

Shape	Tally	Number of Shapes
Circles		
Triangles		
Squares		
Rectangles		

© School District of Hillsborough County. Copying this page without written permission of Metropolitan Teaching and Learning Company is illegal.

HOME CONNECTION: SHAPES AT HOME

Dear Parent or Guardian:

Your child is learning to recognize geometric shapes. Help your child find shapes around the house. Encourage him or her to look for rectangles, squares, triangles, and circles. Help him or her draw and label pictures of the objects.

Rectangles	Squares
Triangles	Circles

© School District of Hillsborough County. Copying this page without written permission of Metropolitan Teaching and Learning Company is illegal.

Name _____

Shapes on the Move

WHERE ARE THEY GOING?

Start With	Action	Prediction	Actual
	Slide		
	Turn		

Start With	Action	Prediction	Actual
	Flip		
	Flip		

© School District of Hillsborough County. Copying this page without written permission of Metropolitan Teaching and Learning Company is illegal.

Name _____

A FLIP, A SLIDE, AND A TURN

➡ Cut out the shape at the bottom of the page.
On this page, first move the shape to make
a flip over the line. Trace the shape and color
in the squares. Then use the shape to make
a slide and color in the squares.

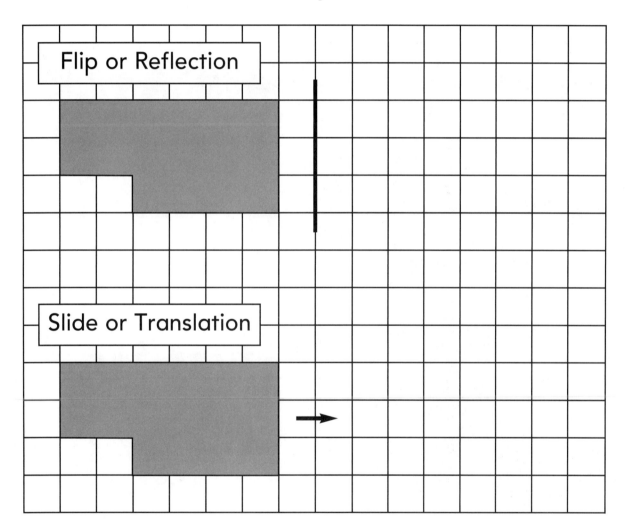

Flip or Reflection

Slide or Translation

Cut out the shape. ⟶

© School District of Hillsborough County. Copying this page without written permission of Metropolitan Teaching and Learning Company is illegal.

Name _____

➡ **Use the shape to make a rotation around the point and color in the squares.**

Rotation or Turn

HOME CONNECTION: SLIDE, FLIP, AND TURN

Dear Parent or Guardian:

Your child has been learning that figures can be moved in different ways. Please help your child by choosing an object, such as an elbow macaroni, that he or she can use to show the moves below.

Slide (or translation) moves a figure in a given direction.

Turn (or rotation) spins a figure around a point.

Flip (or reflection) creates a mirror image.

Trace the object below.

Trace how the object looks now.

Slide

Turn

Flip

© School District of Hillsborough County. Copying this page without written permission of Metropolitan Teaching and Learning Company is illegal.

Name _____

Looking in a Mirror
WHERE'S MY REFLECTION?

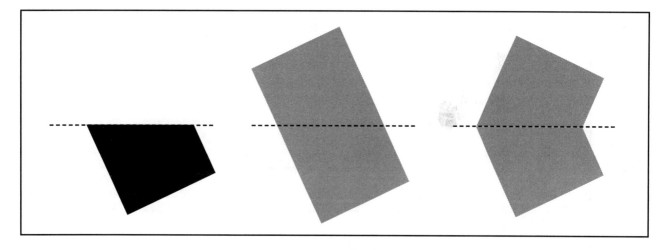

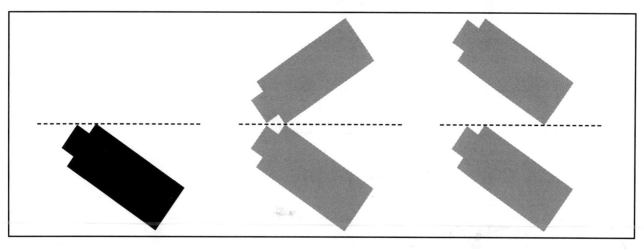

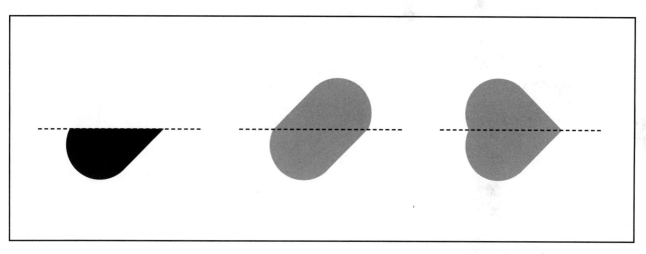

SYMMETRICAL LETTERS

	0 lines	1 line	2 lines	3 lines	4 lines
14					
13					
12					
11					
10					
9					
8					
7					
6					
5					
4					
3					
2					
1					

Number of Letters (vertical axis)

Number of Lines of Symmetry

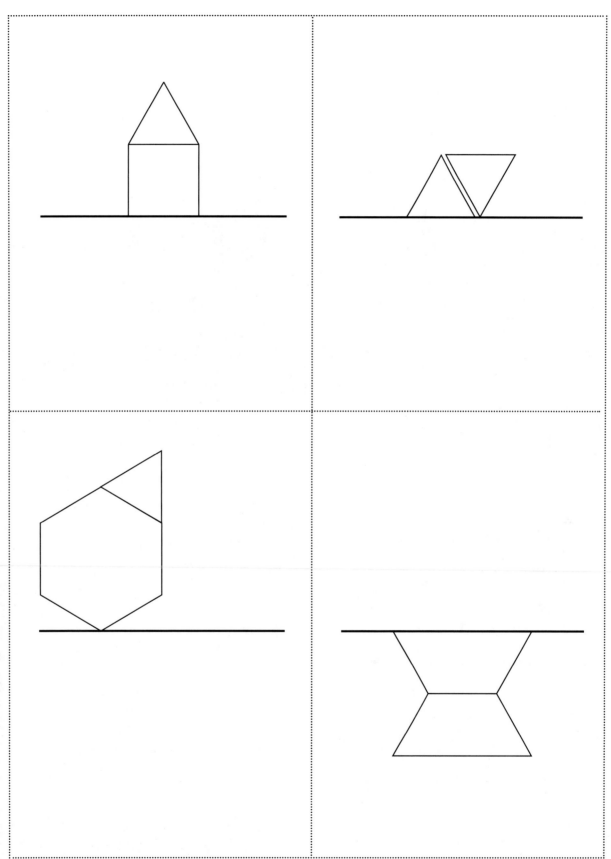

© School District of Hillsborough County. Copying this page without written permission of Metropolitan Teaching and Learning Company is illegal.

"MIRROR MIRROR" GAME CARDS

© School District of Hillsborough County. Copying this page without written permission of Metropolitan Teaching and Learning Company is illegal.

"MIRROR MIRROR" GAME CARDS

HOME CONNECTION: MIRROR IMAGES

Dear Parent or Guardian:

Your child has been learning about symmetry and about drawing lines of symmetry. The line of symmetry of a shape or object is a line that divides the figure into two congruent (identical) halves that are mirror images of each other. Look at the pictures of the two objects below with your child. Talk with him or her about why the object on the left is symmetrical and the object on the right is not.

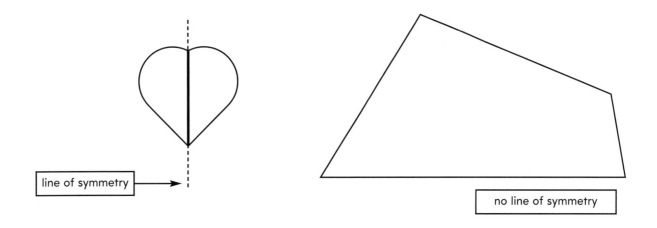

line of symmetry

no line of symmetry

Help your child find a symmetrical object in or near your home. Help him or her draw and label a picture of the object in the box on the other side of this sheet, including the line of symmetry.

© School District of Hillsborough County. Copying this page without written permission of Metropolitan Teaching and Learning Company is illegal.

HOME CONNECTION: MIRROR IMAGES

➡ Find a symmetrical object in or near your home.
Draw and label a picture of the object in the box.
Include the line of symmetry.

Name _____

Captain Geo

WHICH WAY SHOULD I GO?

	A	B	C	D	E	F
8						
7						
6						
5						
4						
3						
2		★				
1						

 right   ⬆ up

⬅ left   down

© School District of Hillsborough County. Copying this page without written permission of Metropolitan Teaching and Learning Company is illegal.

WHICH WAY SHOULD I GO?

	A	B	C	D	E	F
8						
7						
6						
5						
4						
3						
2						
1						

➡ right   ⬆ up

⬅ left   ⬇ down

© School District of Hillsborough County. Copying this page without written permission of Metropolitan Teaching and Learning Company is illegal.

Name _____

CAPTAIN GEO'S TREASURE MAP

8						
7					◆	
6						
5						
4						
3						
2						
1	⛵					
	A	B	C	D	E	F

➡ right   ⬆ up

⬅ left   ⬇ down

Name _____

GRID TIC TAC TOE!

Dear Parent or Guardian:

Your child is learning about coordinate grids in school. Playing Grid Tic Tac Toe with your child is a fun way to reinforce his or her knowledge as well as to develop problem-solving strategies. Each of the nine grid squares is identified by its column letter and its row number. For instance, the center square is B2.

➡ **The first player names a grid square, such as A2, and writes an X in that square. The second player names an empty grid square and writes an O in that square. The player who gets 3 in a row wins!**

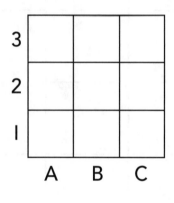
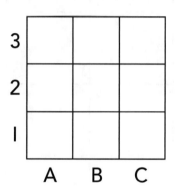
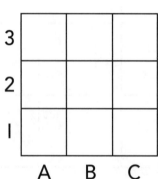
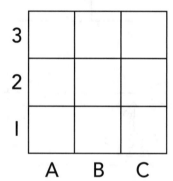
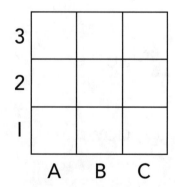
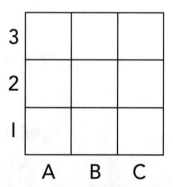

TOPIC 3 Captain Geo

Name _____

Rollin', Rollin', Rollin'

THE SEARCH IS ON!

➡ **List the names of objects that resemble the following figures:**

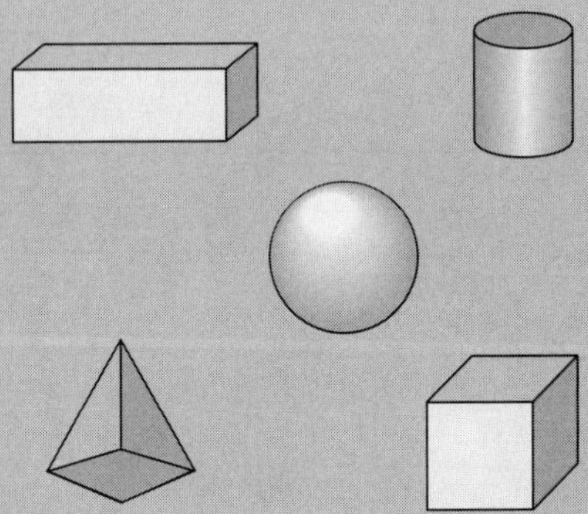	Cube 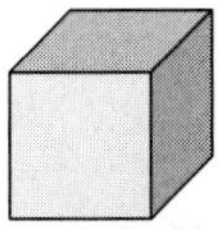
Rectangular Prism 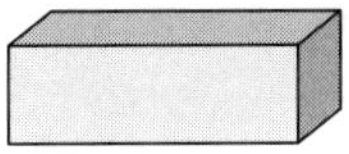	**Sphere** 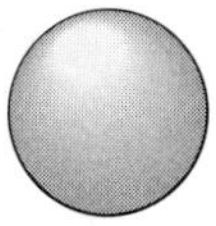
Cylinder 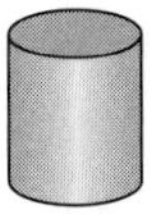	**Square Pyramid** 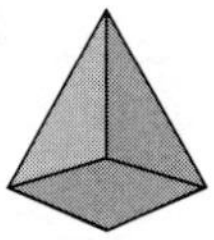

© School District of Hillsborough County. Copying this page without written permission of Metropolitan Teaching and Learning Company is illegal.

HOME CONNECTION:
THE SEARCH IS ON AT HOME!

Dear Parent or Guardian:

Help your child find objects at home that resemble solid figures (cubes, spheres, cones, rectangular prisms, and pyramids). Remind your child that he or she can even look at his or her toys. Have your child draw a picture of one object she or he finds and label it with the name of the solid figure it resembles.

TOPIC 3 Rollin', Rollin', Rollin'

Name _____

Caught in a Net

EDGES AND VERTICES

➡ Create a square-based pyramid and a cube using gumdrops for the vertices and toothpicks for the edges. Count the edges (toothpicks) and vertices (gumdrops) on each shape. Record your results.

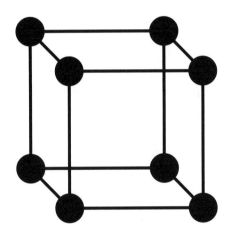

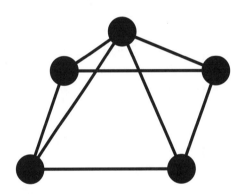

Shape	Edges	Vertices
Square-Based Pyramid		
Cube		

© School District of Hillsborough County. Copying this page without written permission of Metropolitan Teaching and Learning Company is illegal.

HOME CONNECTION: NETS

Dear Parent or Guardian:

Your child has been learning about **nets.** A net is a flat pattern for the surface of a three-dimensional figure, similar to a cardboard box. Help your child find and open up boxes (cereal, cracker, etc.) to see their nets.

Example:

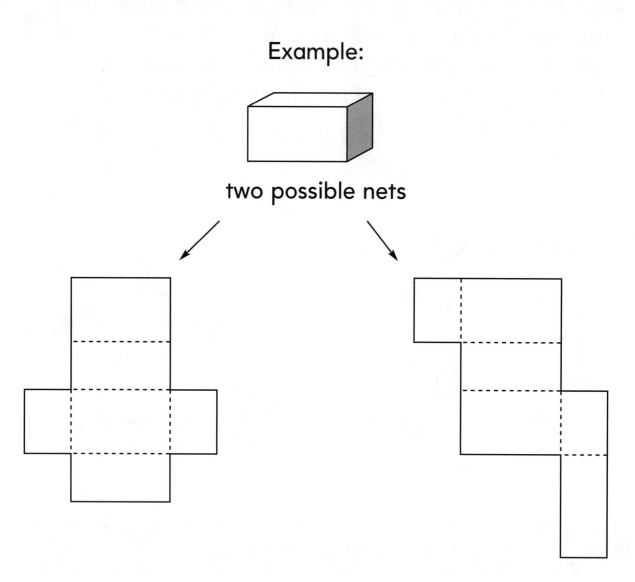

two possible nets

TOPIC 3 Caught in a Net

TOPIC 4

Whole Numbers and Decimals II

© School District of Hillsborough County. Copying this page without written permission of Metropolitan Teaching and Learning Company is illegal.

Name _____

Walking the Line

JUMPING BEANS

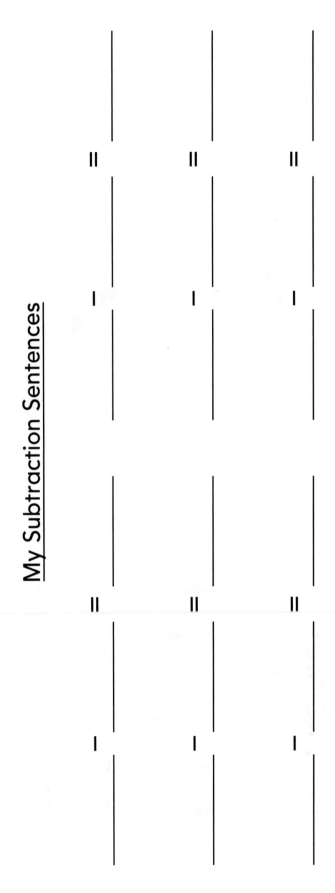

0 1 2 3 4 5 6 7 8 9 10 11 12 13 14 15 16 17

My Subtraction Sentences

	−		=
	−		=
	−		=

	−		=
	−		=
	−		=

WHERE ARE YOU?

➤ **Use the number line to help you solve the riddles.**

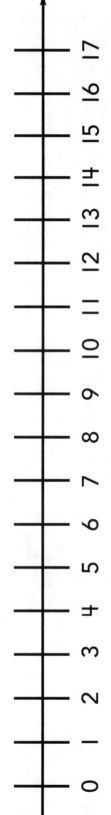

0 1 2 3 4 5 6 7 8 9 10 11 12 13 14 15 16 17

1. Begin at 0.
Move up 7.
Move down 4.

Where are you? _____
Write the subtraction sentence.

_____

2. Begin at 0.
Move up 11.
Move down 5.

Where are you? _____
Write the subtraction sentence.

_____

3. Begin at 0.
Move up 17.
Move down 6.

Where are you? _____
Write the subtraction sentence.

_____

4. Begin at 0.
Move up 13.
Move down 4.

Where are you? _____
Write the subtraction sentence.

_____

Name _____

HOME CONNECTION: LINE RIDDLES

Dear Parent or Guardian:

Your child has been learning how to use number lines to add and subtract. Read the instructions on the other side of this sheet to your child. Then have your child complete the riddles. Finally, have your child show you how he or she used the number line to solve each riddle.

© School District of Hillsborough County. Copying this page without written permission of Metropolitan Teaching and Learning Company is illegal.

HOME CONNECTION: LINE RIDDLES

Use the number line to help you solve the riddles.

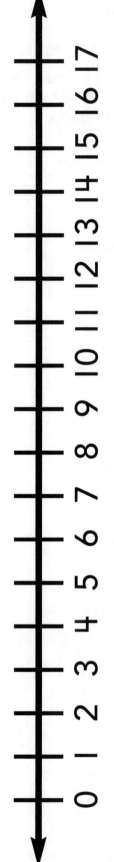

0 1 2 3 4 5 6 7 8 9 10 11 12 13 14 15 16 17

1. Begin at 0.
Move right 5.
Move right 7.
Where are you? _____
Write the addition sentence.

_____

Write your own riddles!

3. Begin at 0.
Move right _____.
Move left _____.
Where are you? _____
Write the subtraction sentence.

_____

2. Begin at 0.
Move right 12.
Move left 6.
Where are you? _____
Write the subtraction sentence.

_____

4. Begin at 0.
Move right _____.
Move right _____.
Where are you? _____
Write the addition sentence.

_____

© School District of Hillsborough County. Copying this page without written permission of Metropolitan Teaching and Learning Company is illegal.

Name _____

Counting Back

COUNTING BACK IS A SNAP

➡ Use snap cubes to help you count back to solve the problems. Write the numbers underneath the snap cubes as you count back. Then write the difference in the subtraction sentence.

1.

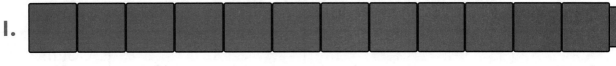

_____ 12

$$12 - 3 = \underline{\quad}$$

2.

_____ 10

$$10 - 2 = \underline{\quad}$$

3.

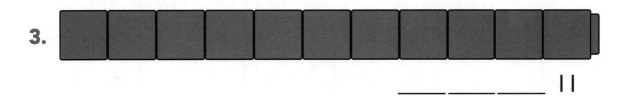

_____ 11

$$11 - 3 = \underline{\quad}$$

SHAKE AND TOSS

➡ Shake the cup and gently toss out the counters. Cover the red counters. Record the number of yellow counters. Find the number of red counters by counting up or back. Record your answer. Ring the strategy you used. Then uncover the red counters and check your answer.

Total Number	Subtract	Number of Yellow	Equals	Number of Red	Strategy Used
12	–	2	=	10	Count Up (Count Back)
12	–		=		Count Up Count Back
12	–		=		Count Up Count Back
12	–		=		Count Up Count Back
12	–		=		Count Up Count Back
12	–		=		Count Up Count Back
12	–		=		Count Up Count Back

TOPIC 4 Counting Back

© School District of Hillsborough County. Copying this page without written permission of Metropolitan Teaching and Learning Company is illegal.

Name _____

COUNT UP OR COUNT BACK?

10 − 2 = ____

Count Up

Count Back

15 − 1 = ____

Count Up

Count Back

9 − 6 = ____

Count Up

Count Back

11 − 7 = ____

Count Up

Count Back

5 − 1 = ____

Count Up

Count Back

18 − 2 = ____

Count Up

Count Back

14 − 9 = ____

Count Up

Count Back

7 − 6 = ____

Count Up

Count Back

© School District of Hillsborough County. Copying this page without written permission of Metropolitan Teaching and Learning Company is illegal.

Name _____

SAMANTHA'S BIRTHDAY PARTY

Samantha is having a birthday party and needs your help counting the items she has.

1. Samantha had 8 party hats, but she played with one and ripped it. How many party hats are left?

   _____ − _____ = _____   _____ party hats

2. Samantha bought some candy and toys for the piñata. She bought 14 yo-yos. Only 10 yo-yos fit in the piñata. How many yo-yos are left?

   _____ − _____ = _____   _____ yo-yos

3. Samantha's friend Zack brought 9 balloons to decorate. He accidentally popped 1 balloon as he came in the house. How many balloons are left?

   _____ − _____ = _____   _____ balloons

4. Samantha is giving away bottles of bubbles as prizes. She has 8 bottles of bubbles. She gives away 3. How many bottles does she have left?

   _____ − _____ = _____   _____ bottles

HOME CONNECTION: TAKE A CARD

Dear Parent or Guardian:

Your child is learning to count back to subtract. For Take a Card your child needs a deck of cards with the kings, queens, and jacks removed. Aces count as 1. Read the following directions with your child and make sure he or she understands them. Let him or her share his or her results with you before bringing them back to school.

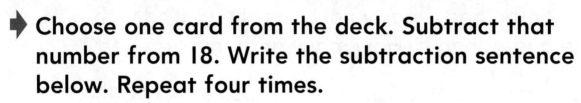 **Choose one card from the deck. Subtract that number from 18. Write the subtraction sentence below. Repeat four times.**

1. _____ — _____ = _____

2. _____ — _____ = _____

3. _____ — _____ = _____

4. _____ — _____ = _____

Name _____

Balance Me!

BALANCE IT!

➡ Use a balance scale and snap cubes. Find the missing addends. Then complete each number sentence.

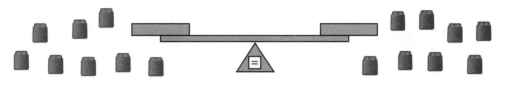

$7 = 2 + \boxed{}$

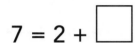 $= \boxed{}\ + ?$

$\boxed{} + 1 = 4$

$? + \boxed{} = \boxed{}$

$4 + \boxed{} = 8$

$8 = \boxed{} + 2$

$5 = \boxed{} + 3$

$6 = 3 + \boxed{}$

$\boxed{} + 1 = 6$

$8 + \boxed{} = 9$

$9 = 5 + \boxed{}$

$\boxed{} + 1 = 7$

© School District of Hillsborough County. Copying this page without written permission of Metropolitan Teaching and Learning Company is illegal.

Name _____

0	1	2	2
3	3	4	4
5	5	6	6
7	7	8	9

© School District of Hillsborough County. Copying this page without written permission of Metropolitan Teaching and Learning Company is illegal.

HOME CONNECTION: FINDING ADDENDS

Dear Parent or Guardian:

Your child has been learning about finding missing addends. Addends are the numbers that are added together in an addition sentence. For example, in the addition sentence 3 + 2 = 5, the numbers 3 and 2 are the addends.

Read the instructions and the problems on the other side of this sheet aloud to your child. Help your child come up with the first addend in each problem. Have him or her use whole numbers. For example, if your child's school day is $6\frac{1}{2}$ hours, have him or her use 7 hours in the problem. Then have your child complete the page. Have your child share the finished page with you.

© School District of Hillsborough County. Copying this page without written permission of Metropolitan Teaching and Learning Company is illegal.

HOME CONNECTION: FINDING ADDENDS

➡ **Complete the following questions based on data you collect at home.**

1. How many more teeth do you need to lose to have lost 10 teeth?

   _____ $+$ ☐ $= 10$
   number of teeth you have lost

2. How many more hours would you need to sleep each night if you wanted to sleep 15 hours each night?

   _____ $+$ ☐ $= 15$
   number of hours you sleep

3. How many more hours would you spend in school each day if the school day were 10 hours long?

   _____ $+$ ☐ $= 10$
   number of hours in your school day

4. How many more times a day would you need to brush your teeth if you wanted to brush your teeth 5 times each day?

   _____ $+$ ☐ $= 5$
   number of times you brush your teeth each day

All Aboard

THE NUMBER TRAIN

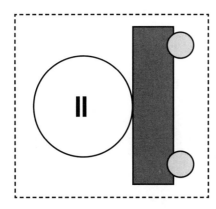

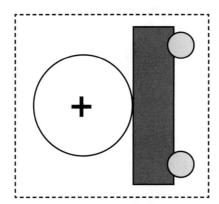

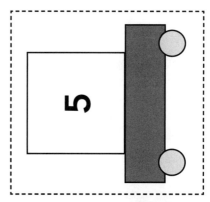

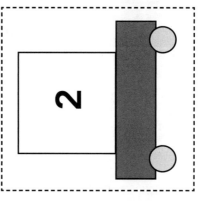

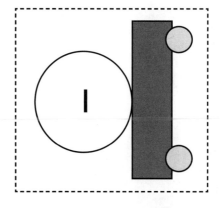

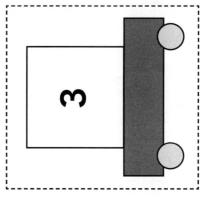

© School District of Hillsborough County. Copying this page without written permission of Metropolitan Teaching and Learning Company is illegal.

© School District of Hillsborough County. Copying this page without written permission of Metropolitan Teaching and Learning Company is illegal.

ON TRACK

➡ Use the numbers in the smoke to make two addition sentences and two subtraction sentences.

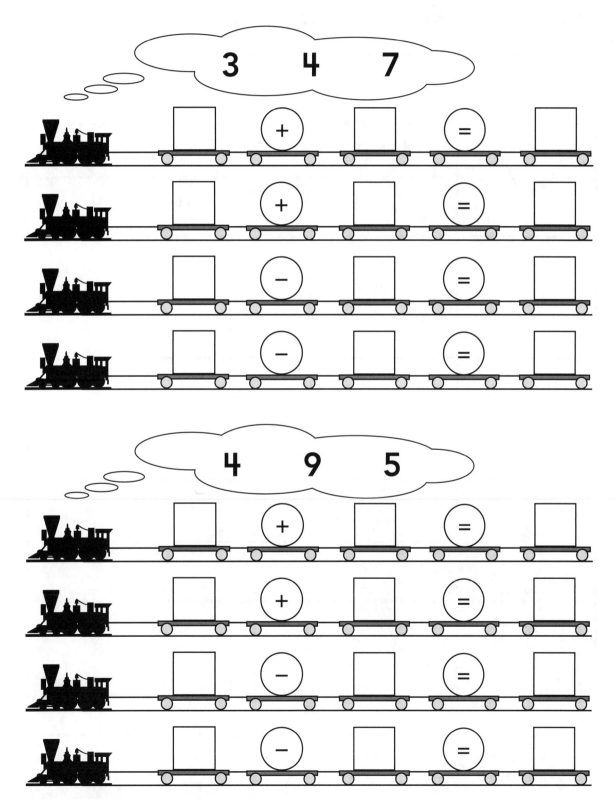

ROLL IT, ROLL IT, ROLL IT

➡ Roll two dice. Write two addition sentences using the two numbers as the addends. Then write two related subtraction sentences. Roll again and make a new fact family.

Numbers Rolled	Fact Family	
4, 6	4 + 6 = 10	6 + 4 = 10
	10 − 4 = 6	10 − 6 = 4

© School District of Hillsborough County. Copying this page without written permission of Metropolitan Teaching and Learning Company is illegal.

Name _____

HOME CONNECTION: FACT FAMILY GAME

Dear Parent or Guardian:

Your child has been learning all about Fact Families.

Play the <u>Fact Family Game</u> with your child. Cut out the number cards on the other side of this sheet. Place them face down on a flat surface. Player 1 draws 2 cards. He or she writes the two addition sentences and the two related subtraction sentences on a sheet of paper. For example, if a player chooses the numbers 2 and 4, he or she would write the following addition and subtraction sentences:

$2 + 4 = 6$ $6 - 4 = 2$

$4 + 2 = 6$ $6 - 2 = 4$

If a player can write all 4 sentences, he or she keeps the cards. If not, the cards are returned. Then the next player takes a turn. When all the cards have been used, the player with the most cards wins.

HOME CONNECTION: FACT FAMILY GAME

1	2	3	4	5	6
1	2	3	4	5	6
1	2	3	4	5	6
1	2	3	4	5	6

© School District of Hillsborough County. Copying this page without written permission of Metropolitan Teaching and Learning Company is illegal.

Super Models

PART/PART/WHOLE

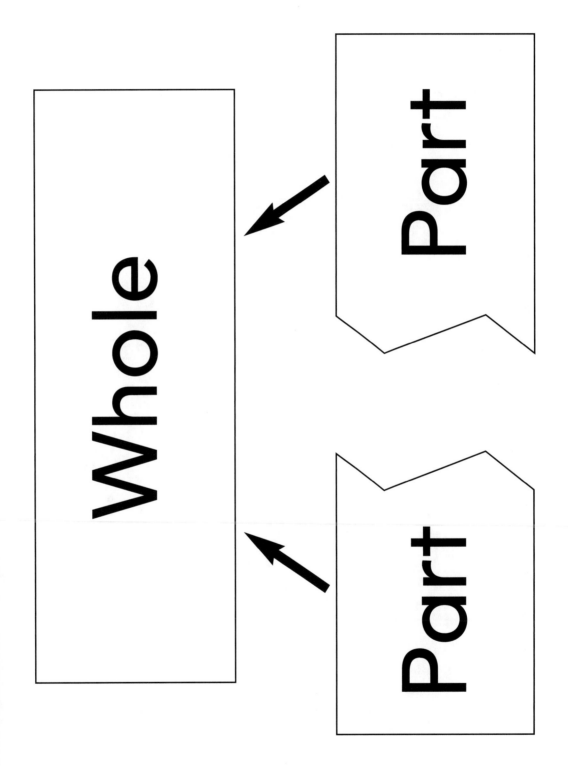

PUT THE PARTS TOGETHER

➡ **Use the model to help solve the problems.**

1. One Monday, Lorie earned $2 for baby-sitting. Later that day, she earned $4 for mopping the floor. How much money did Lorie earn altogether?

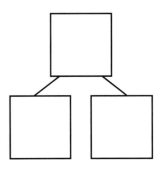

_____

2. Zachary found 12 checkers. There were 6 black checkers, and the rest were red. How many red checkers did he find?

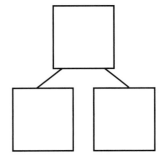

_____

3. There were 7 large gum balls and 5 extra-large gum balls for sale. If Mr. Gumble sold all of the gum balls, how many gum balls did he sell?

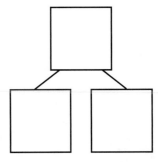

_____

4. Susan bought 9 pink gum balls and some yellow gum balls. Susan has 15 gum balls altogether. How many yellow gum balls does she have?

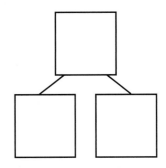

_____

© School District of Hillsborough County. Copying this page without written permission of Metropolitan Teaching and Learning Company is illegal.

© School District of Hillsborough County. Copying this page without written permission of Metropolitan Teaching and Learning Company is illegal.

Name _____

SUPER MODEL MATCH MISSING NUMBER CARDS

3	4
5	7
8	10
11	12
13	17

SUPER MODEL MATCH PROBLEM CARDS

16 ☐ / 9	☐ 2 / 8
7 4 / ☐	14 ☐ / 9
☐ 8 / 5	☐ 8 / 9
☐ 8 / 3	☐ 6 / 6
☐ 8 / 0	12 ☐ / 8

© School District of Hillsborough County. Copying this page without written permission of Metropolitan Teaching and Learning Company is illegal.

© School District of Hillsborough County. Copying this page without written permission of Metropolitan Teaching and Learning Company is illegal.

Name _____

HOME CONNECTION: MISSING PARTS

Dear Parent or Guardian:

Your child has been learning how to find a missing number in an addition model. Your child has learned that the number in the top box of the model is equal to the sum of the numbers in the bottom two boxes.

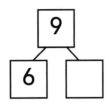

In this example, your child can identify that the missing number is 3. Read the intructions on the other side of this page aloud to your child. Then have your child complete the page. Have your child share the finished page with you and then return it to class.

HOME CONNECTION: MISSING PARTS

1.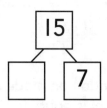

2.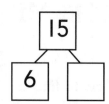

3.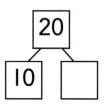

4.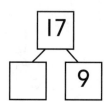

5.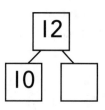

6.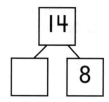

7. Explain how you were able to find each missing part.

_____

_____

_____

_____

_____

_____

_____

TOPIC 4 Super Models

© School District of Hillsborough County. Copying this page without written permission of Metropolitan Teaching and Learning Company is illegal.

Name _____

To 100

SHOW 100

1	2	3	4	5	6	7	8	9	10
11	12	13	14	15	16	17	18	19	20
21	22	23	24	25	26	27	28	29	30
31	32	33	34	35	36	37	38	39	40
41	42	43	44	45	46	47	48	49	50

SUMS AND DIFFERENCES

➡ Write the sum or difference.

1. 17 + 10 = _____

2. 33 − 2 = _____

3. 24 − 10 = _____

4. 15 + 3 = _____

5. 60 + 20 = _____

6. 87 − 4 = _____

7. 99 + 1 = _____

8. 63 − 19 = _____

9. 35 + 5 = _____

10. 42 − 11 = _____

11. 28 − 2 = _____

12. 61 + 30 = _____

13. 5 + 12 = _____

14. 30 + 30 = _____

© School District of Hillsborough County. Copying this page without written permission of Metropolitan Teaching and Learning Company is illegal.

Name _____

HOME CONNECTION: BUILDING 100

Dear Parent or Guardian:

Your child has been learning how to use and complete a hundreds chart. Have your child complete the hundreds chart on the other side of this sheet by finding the missing numbers at the bottom of the page and putting them in their proper places in the chart. Suggest that they cross off each number as they put it in the chart.

HOME CONNECTION: BUILDING 100

Use the missing numbers to complete the hundreds chart.

1	2		4	5	6		8	9	10
	12	13		15	16	17		19	
21	22	23	24		26	27	28		30
31	32	33	34	35		37	38	39	
	42	43	44	45		47	48	49	50
	52	53	54		56	57	58	59	
61	62		64	65	66	67		69	70
	72	73	74	75	76	77		79	
81	82		84		86	87	88	89	90
	92	93	94	95	96	97	98		

MISSING NUMBERS

78	20	51	11	99
83	29	60	68	3
91	55	36	18	100
41	14	25	40	63
71	85	7	46	80

Missing Parts

FILLING IN THE BLANKS

➡ Fill in the missing numbers. The sums are on top. The addends are on the bottom. Some boxes have more than one solution.

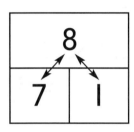 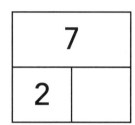 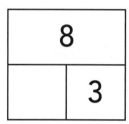

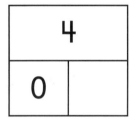 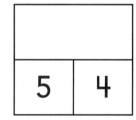 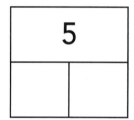

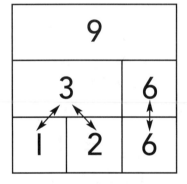 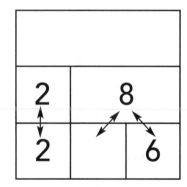 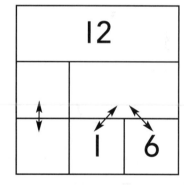

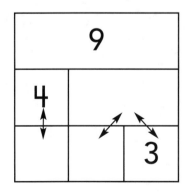 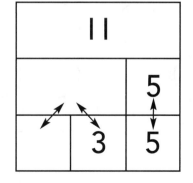 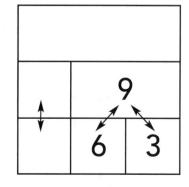

© School District of Hillsborough County. Copying this page without written permission of Metropolitan Teaching and Learning Company is illegal.

COUNTERS TO TEN

➡️ Use your two-color counters to find different pairs of addends that total ten. Color the circles to match your counters. Finish each number sentence.

_____ + _____ = 10

_____ + _____ = 10

_____ + _____ = 10

_____ + _____ = 10

_____ + _____ = 10

_____ + _____ = 10

_____ + _____ = 10

_____ + _____ = 10

TOPIC 4 Missing Parts

© School District of Hillsborough County. Copying this page without written permission of Metropolitan Teaching and Learning Company is illegal.

Name _____

HOME CONNECTION: COLOR TO TEN

Dear Parent or Guardian:

Your child has been learning all the different ways to make ten. Read the instructions on the next page aloud to your child. Then have your child complete the page. Have your child share the finished page with you. The first one is done for you as an example.

HOME CONNECTION: COLOR TO TEN

➡ Color some of the circles in each box one color.
Color the rest of the circles another color. Then finish
each number sentence. The first one is done for you.

● ● ● ○ ○ ○ ○ ○ ○ ○ __3__ + __7__ = 10	○ ○ ○ ○ ○ ○ ○ ○ ○ ○ _____ + _____ = 10
○ ○ ○ ○ ○ ○ ○ ○ ○ ○ _____ + _____ = 10	○ ○ ○ ○ ○ ○ ○ ○ ○ ○ _____ + _____ = 10
○ ○ ○ ○ ○ ○ ○ ○ ○ ○ _____ + _____ = 10	○ ○ ○ ○ ○ ○ ○ ○ ○ ○ _____ + _____ = 10
○ ○ ○ ○ ○ ○ ○ ○ ○ ○ _____ + _____ = 10	○ ○ ○ ○ ○ ○ ○ ○ ○ ○ _____ + _____ = 10

TOPIC 4 Missing Parts

Beans, Beans, Beans

SPIN FOR BEANS!

➡ Use a paper clip and a pencil
to make a spinner.
Spin one time.
Take that many beans.
Spin again.
Take that many beans.
Organize beans into groups of 10.
Record how many tens and
how many ones.

Spins	Number	Picture	Tens and Ones
Spin 1	7	●●●●●●●○○○ ○○○	_1_ tens _3_ ones
Spin 2	6		
Spin 1			___ tens ___ ones
Spin 2			
Spin 1			___ tens ___ ones
Spin 2			
Spin 1			___ tens ___ ones
Spin 2			
Spin 1			___ tens ___ ones
Spin 2			

© School District of Hillsborough County. Copying this page without written permission of Metropolitan Teaching and Learning Company is illegal.

Tens

Ones

TENS AND ONES

➡️ Cut out and use the cards to play a game.

2 tens	3 ones	1 ten	2 ones
4 tens	2 ones	2 tens	4 ones
3 tens	3 ones	4 tens	4 ones
3 tens	2 ones	2 tens	1 one
1 ten	4 ones	4 tens	1 one
3 tens	4 ones	4 tens	3 ones
1 ten	0 ones	0 tens	1 one
5 tens	3 ones	3 tens	5 ones

© School District of Hillsborough County. Copying this page without written permission of Metropolitan Teaching and Learning Company is illegal.

DRAWING FOR RODS

Card One	Card Two	Total	Total
<u>2</u> tens <u>3</u> ones ⬚⬚⬚	<u>l</u> tens <u>2</u> ones ⬚⬚	<u>3</u> tens <u>5</u> ones ⬚⬚⬚⬚⬚	<u>35</u>
__ tens __ ones	__ tens __ ones	__ tens __ ones	__
__ tens __ ones	__ tens __ ones	__ tens __ ones	__
__ tens __ ones	__ tens __ ones	__ tens __ ones	__
__ tens __ ones	__ tens __ ones	__ tens __ ones	__
__ tens __ ones	__ tens __ ones	__ tens __ ones	__

© School District of Hillsborough County. Copying this page without written permission of Metropolitan Teaching and Learning Company is illegal.

TOPIC 4 Beans, Beans, Beans

HOME CONNECTION: HOW MANY TENS IN YOUR NAME?

Dear Parent or Guardian:

Your child is learning to write numbers as tens and ones. Please read your child the directions below and help him or her spell family or friends' names.

➡ **Write your first and last name. Do not leave a space between the names. Count the number of letters in your name. Write the amount as tens and ones. Do the same for three other family members or friends.**

— — — — — — — — — — — —

— — — — — — — — — — —

— — — — — — — — — — — —

__ tens __ ones

— — — — — — — — — — — —

— — — — — — — — — — —

— — — — — — — — — — —

__ tens __ ones

— — — — — — — — — — — —

— — — — — — — — — — — —

— — — — — — — — — — —

__ tens __ ones

— — — — — — — — — — — —

— — — — — — — — — — —

— — — — — — — — — — — —

__ tens __ ones

Give Me Five

NICKEL BY NICKEL

Nickel by Nickel Score Card

Number of Nickels	Number of Cents
1	5
2	10
3	___
4	___
5	___
6	___
7	35
8	___
9	___
___	___
___	___
___	___
___	___
___	___
___	80
___	___
___	___
___	___
___	___

Number of Nickels this Turn	Total Number of Nickels	Total Number of Cents

© School District of Hillsborough County. Copying this page without written permission of Metropolitan Teaching and Learning Company is illegal.

HOME CONNECTION: NICKEL BY NICKEL

Dear Parent or Guardian:

Your child is learning to count by fives by playing the game <u>Nickel by Nickel</u>. Please play a game with your child. You may use nickels or beans or macaroni to represent nickels.

➡ **Roll a die to find out how many nickels to take. Record the number of nickels taken, the player's total number of nickels, and the total value of all nickels on the score card. If necessary, refer to the nickel value chart completed in school on the other side of this page. Play until someone reaches $1.00.**

Nickel by Nickel Score Card

Number of Nickels this Turn	Total Number of Nickels	Total Number of Cents

Nickel by Nickel Score Card

Number of Nickels this Turn	Total Number of Nickels	Total Number of Cents

What Do You Think?

SKIP-COUNTING CHARTS

➡ Color the following skip-counting patterns.

Skip-Count by 2s

0	1	2	3	4	5	6	7	8	9
10	11	12	13	14	15	16	17	18	19
20	21	22	23	24	25	26	27	28	29
30	31	32	33	34	35	36	37	38	39
40	41	42	43	44	45	46	47	48	49
50	51	52	53	54	55	56	57	58	59
60	61	62	63	64	65	66	67	68	69
70	71	72	73	74	75	76	77	78	79
80	81	82	83	84	85	86	87	88	89
90	91	92	93	94	95	96	97	98	99

Skip-Count by 3s

0	1	2	3	4	5	6	7	8	9
10	11	12	13	14	15	16	17	18	19
20	21	22	23	24	25	26	27	28	29
30	31	32	33	34	35	36	37	38	39
40	41	42	43	44	45	46	47	48	49
50	51	52	53	54	55	56	57	58	59
60	61	62	63	64	65	66	67	68	69
70	71	72	73	74	75	76	77	78	79
80	81	82	83	84	85	86	87	88	89
90	91	92	93	94	95	96	97	98	99

Skip-Count by 4s

0	1	2	3	4	5	6	7	8	9
10	11	12	13	14	15	16	17	18	19
20	21	22	23	24	25	26	27	28	29
30	31	32	33	34	35	36	37	38	39
40	41	42	43	44	45	46	47	48	49
50	51	52	53	54	55	56	57	58	59
60	61	62	63	64	65	66	67	68	69
70	71	72	73	74	75	76	77	78	79
80	81	82	83	84	85	86	87	88	89
90	91	92	93	94	95	96	97	98	99

Skip-Count by 5s

0	1	2	3	4	5	6	7	8	9
10	11	12	13	14	15	16	17	18	19
20	21	22	23	24	25	26	27	28	29
30	31	32	33	34	35	36	37	38	39
40	41	42	43	44	45	46	47	48	49
50	51	52	53	54	55	56	57	58	59
60	61	62	63	64	65	66	67	68	69
70	71	72	73	74	75	76	77	78	79
80	81	82	83	84	85	86	87	88	89
90	91	92	93	94	95	96	97	98	99

© School District of Hillsborough County. Copying this page without written permission of Metropolitan Teaching and Learning Company is illegal.

NUMBER LINES

➡ Look for a pattern. Finish each number line by writing the correct numeral below each point.

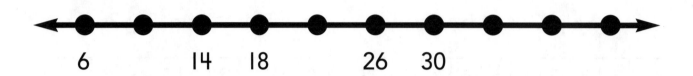

6   14   18   26   30

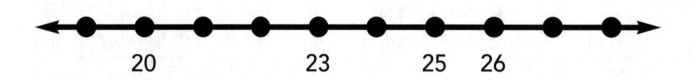

20   23   25   26

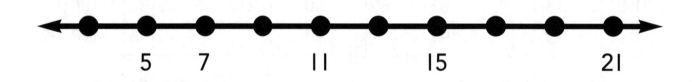

5   7   11   15   21

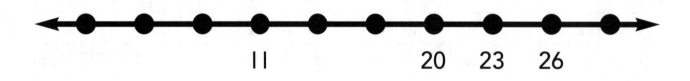

11   20   23   26

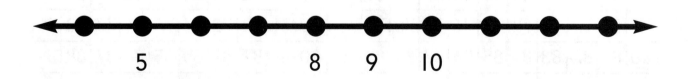

5   8   9   10

© School District of Hillsborough County. Copying this page without written permission of Metropolitan Teaching and Learning Company is illegal.

SEE THE PATTERN?

➡️ **Solve the following problems using number patterns. Use the number lines to help you solve.**

1. Your goal is to read 30 books. You read 3 books each day. How many days will it take you to reach your goal? _____ days

2. Your grandpa gives you a bag of raisins. There are 55 raisins in the bag. You eat 5 raisins the first day and 5 more each day after that. How many days does it take you to eat the entire bag? _____ days

3. For doing a good deed, your teacher gives you a jar with 15 marbles inside. She says she will put 2 more marbles in the jar every time she notices another good deed. You will have a popcorn party when there are at least 40 marbles in the jar. How many more good deeds will she need to see for you to earn the party? _____ good deeds

HOME CONNECTION: HOW LONG DID IT TAKE?

Dear Parent or Guardian:

Your child is learning to skip-count. This home project lets children use this skill for a real-life problem. Please help your child buy a bag or box of an inexpensive snack your family enjoys (crackers, baby carrots, or grapes, for example). Read the following instructions with your child and, if necessary, daily remind him or her to carry out the project.

1. Count the number of pieces of the snack. Record the total amount in the first space on the chart below.

2. Give each member of your family one piece of the snack each day.

3. How many pieces will your family eat every day? _____

4. Each day, subtract that amount from the total of the remaining pieces. Continue until no pieces are left.

5. Record the number of days it takes your family to finish the snack. _____

6. Return this page to school when the snack is gone.

	Day 1	Day 2	Day 3	Day 4	Day 5	Day 6	Day 7
Number of pieces.	_____	_____	_____	_____	_____	_____	_____
Number of pieces eaten today.	_____	_____	_____	_____	_____	_____	_____

	Day 8	Day 9	Day 10	Day 11	Day 12	Day 13	Day 14
Number of pieces.	_____	_____	_____	_____	_____	_____	_____
Number of pieces eaten today.	_____	_____	_____	_____	_____	_____	_____

TOPIC 5

Measurement

Name _____

Measurement

WHAT'S MY MEASUREMENT?

Item to Measure	Estimate: How many _____?	Measure: How many inches?
Pencil		
Glue		
Crayon		
Desk		
Paper		

© School District of Hillsborough County. Copying this page without written permission of Metropolitan Teaching and Learning Company is illegal.

ABOUT HOW LONG?

➡ **About how long do you think each real object is? Ring the best answer.**

Shorter than I foot

Longer than I foot

Shorter than I foot

Longer than I foot

Shorter than I foot

Longer than I foot

Shorter than I foot

Longer than I foot

Shorter than I foot

Longer than I foot

Shorter than I foot

Longer than I foot

Shorter than I foot

Longer than I foot

Shorter than I foot

Longer than I foot

© School District of Hillsborough County. Copying this page without written permission of Metropolitan Teaching and Learning Company is illegal.

Name _____

ABOUT FEET

about one foot	about one foot	folder	football
greater than one foot	greater than one foot	chalkboard	height of a table
less than one foot	less than one foot	paper clip	eraser
about one foot	about one foot	pad of paper	door
less than one foot	less than one foot	crayon	my foot
greater than one foot	greater than one foot	height of a person	12-inch ruler

TOGETHER

© School District of Hillsborough County. Copying this page without written permission of Metropolitan Teaching and Learning Company is illegal.

TOGETHER GAME BOARD

Start

Finish

© School District of Hillsborough County. Copying this page without written permission of Metropolitan Teaching and Learning Company is illegal.

HOME CONNECTION: BIG FOOT HUNT!

Dear Parent or Guardian:

Help your child find items in your house that are less than one foot long, about one foot long, and greater than one foot long. Your child can record his or her findings in the chart below with a picture or words.

Less Than One Foot

About One Foot

Greater Than One Foot

It's a Cm-Inch

HOW MANY THUMBPRINTS?

➡ Predict how many thumbprints long each item is.
Then use your thumbprint ruler to measure the
objects. Record about how many thumbprints
long it is.

Item to Measure	Prediction: How many thumbprints long?	Measurement: Use your thumbprint ruler.
Pencil		
Scissors		
Book		
Desk		
Crayon		

© School District of Hillsborough County. Copying this page without written permission of Metropolitan Teaching and Learning Company is illegal.

IT'S ABOUT INCHES

➡ Predict how many inches long each item is.
   Then use your yard ruler to measure the objects.
   Record about how many inches long each object is.

Item to Measure	Prediction: About how many inches long?	Measurement: About _____ inches
Book		
Table		
Rug		
Paper		

© School District of Hillsborough County. Copying this page without written permission of Metropolitan Teaching and Learning Company is illegal.

Name _____

Glue Here

Glue Here

Glue Here

Glue Here

8   1   2   3

7   15   23   31

6   14   22   30

5   13   21   29

4   12   20   28   36

3   11   19   27   35

2   10   18   26   34

1   9   17   25   33

6   4   2

YARD

© School District of Hillsborough County. Copying this page without written permission of Metropolitan Teaching and Learning Company is illegal.

Name _____

IT'S A CENTIMETER-INCH #2

Glue Here	Glue Here	Glue Here	Glue Here

2 4 6 8

19 39 59 79 99 100

18 38 58 78 98

17 37 57 77 97

16 36 56 76 96

15 35 55 75 95

14 34 54 74 94

13 33 53 73 93

12 32 52 72 92

11 31 51 71 91

10 30 50 70 90

9 29 49 69 89

8 28 48 68 88

7 27 47 67 87

6 26 46 66 86

5 25 45 65 85

4 24 44 64 84

3 23 43 63 83

2 22 42 62 82

1 21 41 61 81

0 0 0 0

© School District of Hillsborough County. Copying this page without written permission of Metropolitan Teaching and Learning Company is illegal.

Name _____

IT'S ABOUT CENTIMETERS

➡ Predict how many centimeters long each item is. Then use your metric ruler to measure the objects. Record about how many centimeters long each object is.

Item to Measure	Prediction: About how many centimeters long?	Measurement: About _____ centimeters
Book		
Table		
Rug		
Paper		

STRING ON

String	Prediction: How many centimeters?	Measurement: Use your meter ruler.
1	_____ cm	_____ cm
2	_____ cm	_____ cm
1 and 2	_____ cm	_____ cm

Length of My 2 Strings	Length of My Partner's 2 Strings	Prediction: How many centimeters altogether?	Measurement: Use your meter ruler.
_____ cm	_____ cm	_____ cm	_____ cm

© School District of Hillsborough County. Copying this page without written permission of Metropolitan Teaching and Learning Company is illegal.

Name _____

HOME CONNECTION: SCAVENGER HUNT

Dear Parent or Guardian:

Your child has been learning all about measuring length. He or she has learned to measure in inches and in centimeters.

Help your child cut out the rulers on the other side of this sheet. Then have him or her go on a scavenger hunt to complete that page.

HOME CONNECTION: SCAVENGER HUNT

➡ Go on a scavenger hunt around your home. Find two things for each measurement.

Measurement	Items
I inch	1. 2.
I centimeter	1. 2.
2 inches	1. 2.
8 centimeters	1. 2.
7 inches	1. 2.
20 centimeters	1. 2.

TOPIC 5 It's a Cm-Inch

Name _____

Weigh to Go

ESTIMATE

Object	Prediction	Measure
	less than 1 pound more than 1 pound 1 pound	less than 1 pound more than 1 pound 1 pound
	less than 1 pound more than 1 pound 1 pound	less than 1 pound more than 1 pound 1 pound
	less than 1 pound more than 1 pound 1 pound	less than 1 pound more than 1 pound 1 pound
	less than 1 pound more than 1 pound 1 pound	less than 1 pound more than 1 pound 1 pound
	less than 1 pound more than 1 pound 1 pound	less than 1 pound more than 1 pound 1 pound

© School District of Hillsborough County. Copying this page without written permission of Metropolitan Teaching and Learning Company is illegal.

MORE, LESS, EQUAL?

Circle <u>more than</u>, <u>less than</u>, or <u>equal to</u> one pound to describe the weight of the object on the right side of each balance.

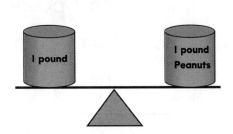

more than   less than   equal to
_____ one pound

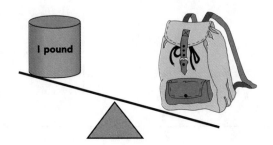

more than   less than   equal to
_____ one pound

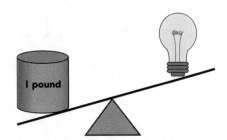

more than   less than   equal to
_____ one pound

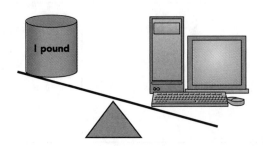

more than   less than   equal to
_____ one pound

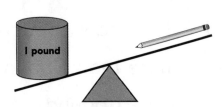

more than   less than   equal to
_____ one pound

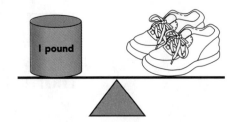

more than   less than   equal to
_____ one pound

HOME CONNECTION: WHAT'S IN A POUND?

Dear Parent or Guardian:

Your child has been learning all about how to weigh things in pounds. To help your child complete the activity on the other side of this sheet, find an item in your house that weighs exactly 1 pound, such as a pound of flour. Have your child use that item to help identify items that weigh more than a pound and less than a pound. Read the instructions on the on the other side of this sheet aloud to your child. Then help your child complete the page.

© School District of Hillsborough County. Copying this page without written permission of Metropolitan Teaching and Learning Company is illegal.

HOME CONNECTION: WHAT'S IN A POUND?

➡ Make a list of five household items that weigh more than a pound, five that weigh less than a pound, and one item that weighs one pound.

More Than a Pound

1. _____
2. _____
3. _____
4. _____
5. _____

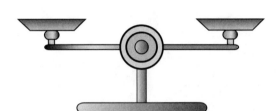

Less Than a Pound

1. _____
2. _____
3. _____
4. _____
5. _____

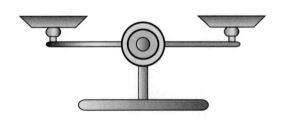

Weighs One Pound

_____

© School District of Hillsborough County. Copying this page without written permission of Metropolitan Teaching and Learning Company is illegal.

Name _____

How Much Does It Hold?

FILL IT UP

Our Container			
Student One		Student Two	
Estimate	Actual	Estimate	Actual

How many handfuls fill the container?

Our Container			
Student One		Student Two	
Estimate	Actual	Estimate	Actual

How many handfuls fill the cup?

How many cups fill the container?

HOW MANY CUPS?

Container	Estimate How many cups do you think it will hold?	Actual How many cups does it hold?
Pint		
Quart		
Half Gallon		
Gallon		

Name _____

HOME CONNECTION: A CUP, MORE OR LESS

Dear Parent or Guardian:

Your child has been learning all about how to measure in cups, pints, quarts, half-gallons, and gallons. To help your child complete the activity on the other side of this sheet, find either a measuring cup or a cup that holds about 8 ounces. Read the instructions on the other side of this sheet aloud to your child. Then help your child complete the page.

© School District of Hillsborough County. Copying this page without written permission of Metropolitan Teaching and Learning Company is illegal.

HOME CONNECTION: A CUP, MORE OR LESS

➡ Make a list of five containers in your home that hold more than a cup, five that hold less than a cup, and one item that holds exactly one cup.

More Than a Cup

1. _____

2. _____

3. _____

4. _____

5. _____

Less Than a Cup

1. _____

2. _____

3. _____

4. _____

5. _____

One Cup

_____

© School District of Hillsborough County. Copying this page without written permission of Metropolitan Teaching and Learning Company is illegal.

Name _____

The Mercury's Rising

WHAT'S THE TEMPERATURE?

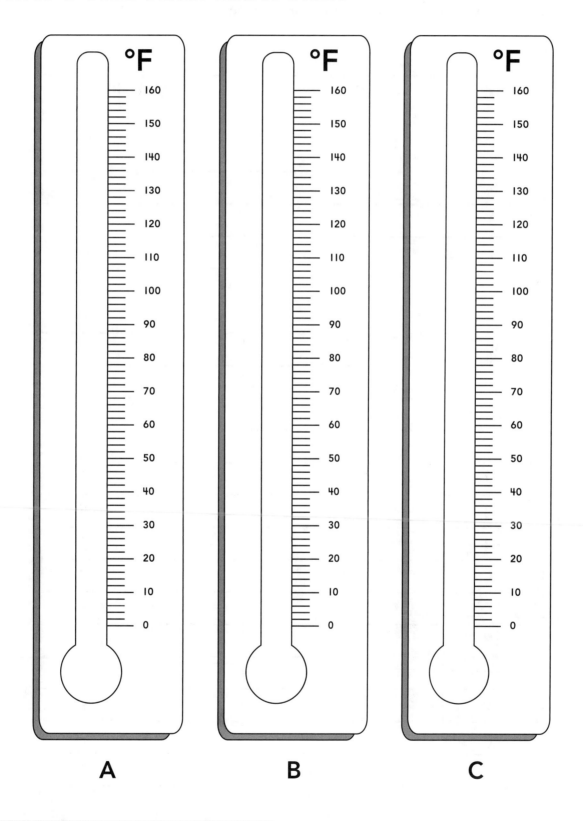

HOME CONNECTION: DAILY TEMPERATURE

Dear Parent or Guardian:

Help your child take the outdoor temperature every day at the same time for three weeks. Have him or her record the date and temperature each day. Then have your child bring the chart to school to share and compare.

Day	Date	Temperature
1		°F
2		°F
3		°F
4		°F
5		°F
6		°F
7		°F
8		°F
9		°F
10		°F
11		°F
12		°F
13		°F
14		°F
15		°F
16		°F
17		°F
18		°F
19		°F
20		°F
21		°F

TOPIC 5 The Mercury's Rising

Clock Works

MY CLOCK

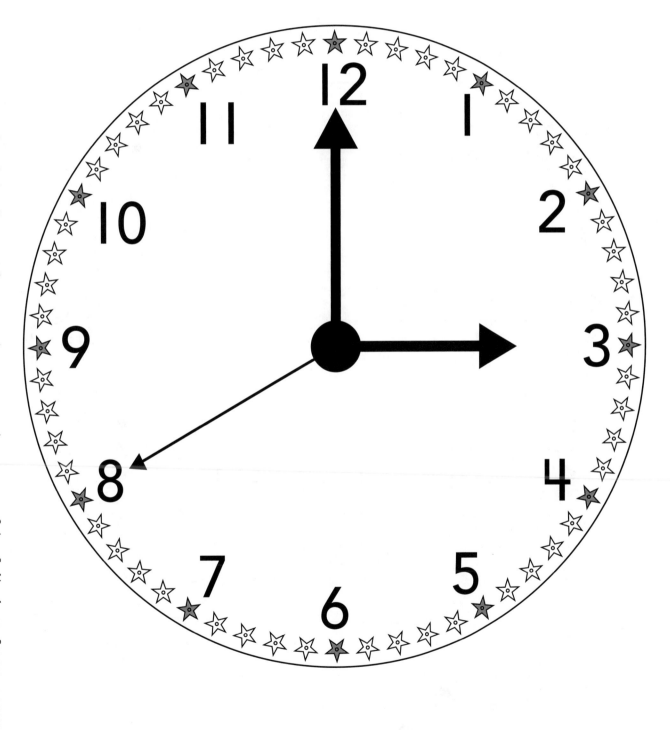

© School District of Hillsborough County. Copying this page without written permission of Metropolitan Teaching and Learning Company is illegal.

MINUTES AND HOURS

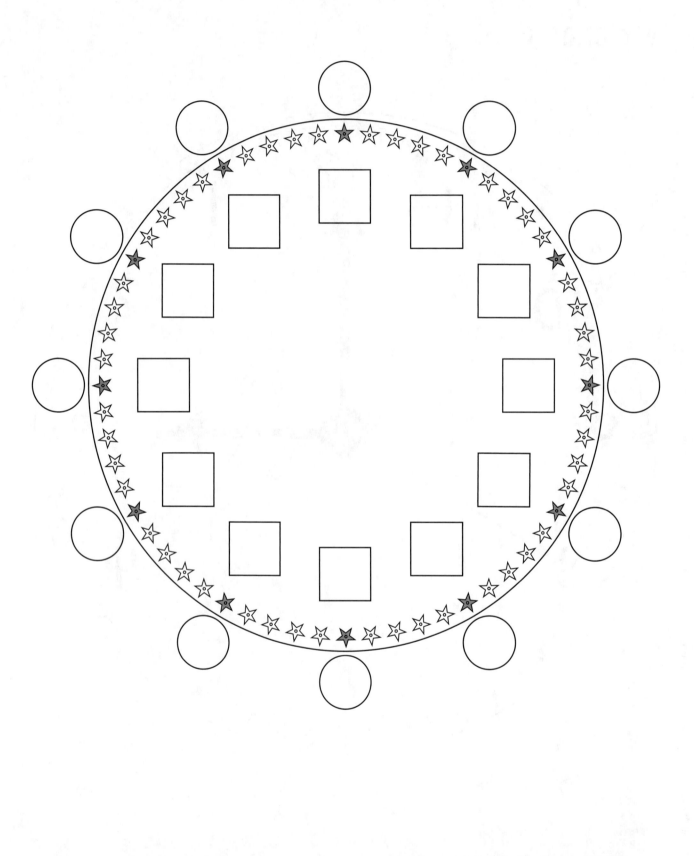

Name _____

HOME CONNECTION: TICK TOCK

Dear Parent or Guardian:

Your child has been learning all about telling time on an analog clock. Read the directions and the questions on the other side of this sheet to your child. Then have your child complete the page and share it with you.

© School District of Hillsborough County. Copying this page without written permission of Metropolitan Teaching and Learning Company is illegal.

HOME CONNECTION: TICK TOCK

➡️ Draw the hands on the clock to show the time you do the activity on a school day.

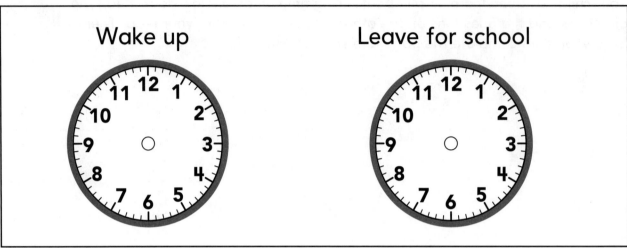

Wake up

Leave for school

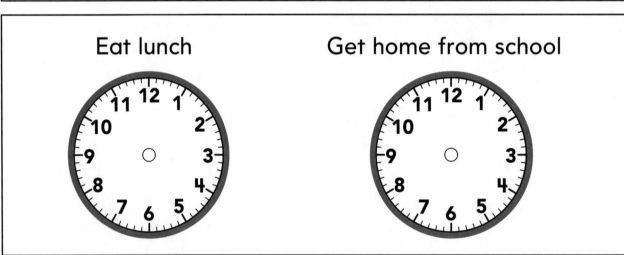

Eat lunch

Get home from school

Eat dinner

Go to bed

TOPIC 5 Clock Works

© School District of Hillsborough County. Copying this page without written permission of Metropolitan Teaching and Learning Company is illegal.

Name _____

Calendar Maker

DECEMBER–MARCH

| 1 | 2 | 3 | 4 | 5 | 6 | 7 | 8 | 9 | 10 | 11 | 12 | 13 | 14 | 15 | Glue Here |
| 16 | 17 | 18 | 19 | 20 | 21 | 22 | 23 | 24 | 25 | 26 | 27 | 28 | 29 | 30 | 31 |

| 1 | 2 | 3 | 4 | 5 | 6 | 7 | 8 | 9 | 10 | 11 | 12 | 13 | 14 | 15 | Glue Here |
| 16 | 17 | 18 | 19 | 20 | 21 | 22 | 23 | 24 | 25 | 26 | 27 | 28 | 29 | 30 | 31 |

| 1 | 2 | 3 | 4 | 5 | 6 | 7 | 8 | 9 | 10 | 11 | 12 | 13 | 14 | 15 | Glue Here |
| 16 | 17 | 18 | 19 | 20 | 21 | 22 | 23 | 24 | 25 | 26 | 27 | 28 | 29 | 30 | 31 |

| 1 | 2 | 3 | 4 | 5 | 6 | 7 | 8 | 9 | 10 | 11 | 12 | 13 | 14 | 15 | Glue Here |
| 16 | 17 | 18 | 19 | 20 | 21 | 22 | 23 | 24 | 25 | 26 | 27 | 28 | 29 | 30 | 31 |

© School District of Hillsborough County. Copying this page without written permission of Metropolitan Teaching and Learning Company is illegal.

Name _____

January

Sunday	Monday	Tuesday	Wednesday	Thursday	Friday	Saturday

March

Sunday	Monday	Tuesday	Wednesday	Thursday	Friday	Saturday

December

Sunday	Monday	Tuesday	Wednesday	Thursday	Friday	Saturday

February

Sunday	Monday	Tuesday	Wednesday	Thursday	Friday	Saturday

Name _____

© School District of Hillsborough County. Copying this page without written permission of Metropolitan Teaching and Learning Company is illegal.

FIFTY DAYS OF GIVEAWAYS

October

Sunday	Monday	Tuesday	Wednesday	Thursday	Friday	Saturday
	1	2	3	4	5	6
7	8	9	10	11	12	13
14	15	16	17	18	19	20
21	22	23	24	25	26	

November

Sunday	Monday	Tuesday	Wednesday	Thursday	Friday	Saturday

December

Sunday	Monday	Tuesday	Wednesday	Thursday	Friday	Saturday

January

Sunday	Monday	Tuesday	Wednesday	Thursday	Friday	Saturday

HOME CONNECTION: NEXT MONTH

Dear Parent or Guardian:

Your child has been learning about the calendar.

The blank calendar below should be dated for <u>next</u> month by your child. Show your child this month's calendar. Do not show any other month. Encourage your child to explain how she or he knows what day next month starts on. Help her or him write the name of the month and the year.

Month: _____

Year: _____

Sunday	Monday	Tuesday	Wednesday	Thursday	Friday	Saturday

TOPIC 5 Calendar Maker

Name _____

Featherweight Competition

MEASURE MATCH

➡ Draw a line to match the unit of measure to the item being measured.

centimeters   school year

miles   body temperature

months   distance between
                                    home and school

°F   liquid in a milk jug

pounds   length of a crayon

hours   amount of sleep

cups   person's weight

© School District of Hillsborough County. Copying this page without written permission of Metropolitan Teaching and Learning Company is illegal.

Name

Event	Estimate		Actual	
Water Run		oz		oz
Clay Dough Roll		cm		cm
Paper Plate Flyer		ft		ft
Cotton Ball Breeze		cm		cm
Feather Flurry		in.		in.
Warm Me Up		°F		°F

Name _____

HOME CONNECTION: WHAT SHOULD I MEASURE?

Dear Parent or Guardian:

Your child has been learning how to use different units of measure. Read the instructions on the other side of this sheet aloud to your child.
Then help your child complete the page.

© School District of Hillsborough County. Copying this page without written permission of Metropolitan Teaching and Learning Company is illegal.

HOME CONNECTION: WHAT SHOULD I MEASURE?

➡ Draw or write at least two things you could measure using each unit of measure.

centimeters	hours
cups	pounds
miles	°F

© School District of Hillsborough County. Copying this page without written permission of Metropolitan Teaching and Learning Company is illegal.

Count the Coins

HOW MUCH?

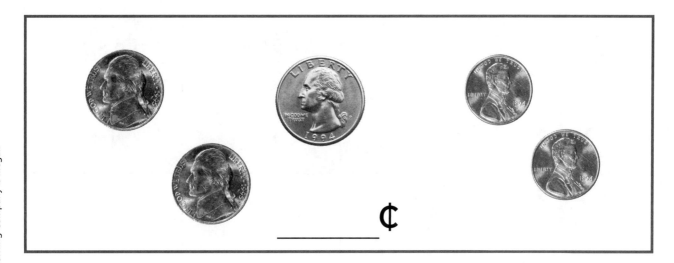

_____ ¢

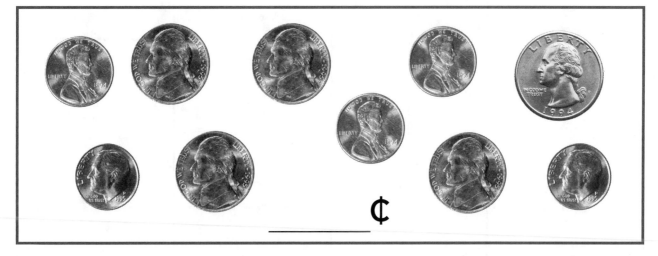

_____ ¢

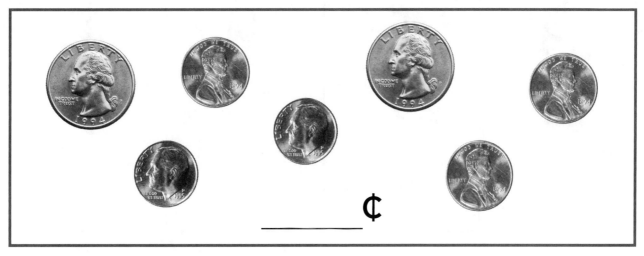

_____ ¢

LETTER COUNT

Quarter	Dime	Nickel	Penny
25¢	10¢	5¢	1¢
a	b	c	d
e	f	g	h
i	j	k	l
m	n	o	p
q	r	s	t
u	v	w	x
y	z		

TOPIC 5 Count the Coins

MONEY WORDS

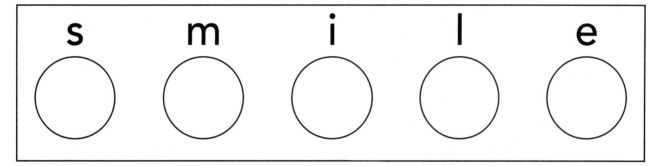

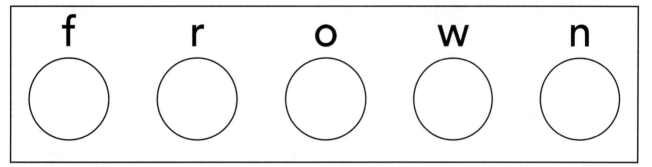

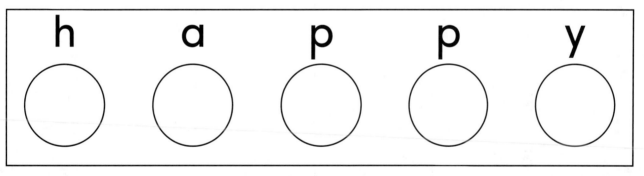

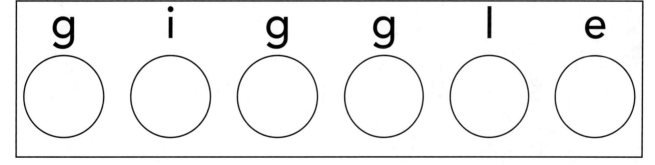

© School District of Hillsborough County. Copying this page without written permission of Metropolitan Teaching and Learning Company is illegal.

HOME CONNECTION: NAME COUNT

Dear Parent or Guardian:

Your child is learning ways to count coins. Please read the directions below and help your child spell the names.

➤ **Write the names of several of your family members. Use the values on the Letter Count chart to find the value of each name.**

TOPIC 5 Count the Coins

TOPIC 6
Fractions

© School District of Hillsborough County. Copying this page without written permission of Metropolitan Teaching and Learning Company is illegal.

Fraction Fish and Other Friends

DRAWING FRACTIONS

➡ Use a ruler to draw a straight line between the marks. How many parts did you show for each circle?

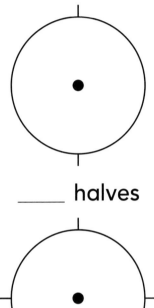

_____ halves

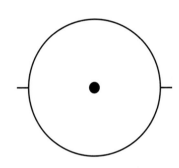

_____ halves

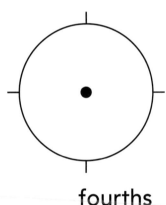

_____ fourths

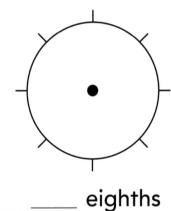

_____ eighths

➡ Use your ruler to show how you folded and cut squares into halves and fourths.

_____ halves

_____ fourths

FRACTION PICTURES

➡ Use your fraction pieces to make a picture.
Glue the pieces to the paper.
Tell how many of each sized piece you used.
Write the numerator for each fractional value.

I used _____ whole circles.

I used _____ of the circle halves. $\dfrac{}{2}$

I used _____ of the circle fourths. $\dfrac{}{4}$

I used _____ of the circle eighths. $\dfrac{}{8}$

Name _____

HOME CONNECTION: COLORFUL FRACTIONS

Dear Parent or Guardian:

Your child has been learning all about fractions. He or she has learned how to cut circles and squares into halves, quarters, and eighths. Read the instructions on the other side of this sheet aloud to your child. Then have your child complete the page. Have your child share the completed page with you.

© School District of Hillsborough County. Copying this page without written permission of Metropolitan Teaching and Learning Company is illegal.

HOME CONNECTION: COLORFUL FRACTIONS

➡ **Follow the directions under each shape.**

1.

Color one half of the square red.

2.

Color one fourth of the square yellow.

3.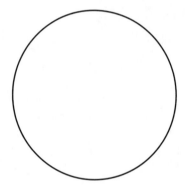

Color one half of the circle red.

4.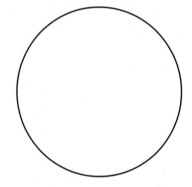

Color one fourth of the circle yellow.

5.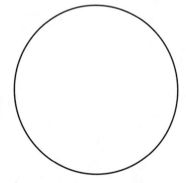

Color one half of the circle red.

6.

Color one fourth of the square yellow.

Set to Party

SHAKE AND SHOW

Total Number of Counters	Color of Counters	Number of Color Counters	Fraction: $\frac{Color}{Total}$
	Red		____
	Yellow		____
	Red		____
	Yellow		____
	Red		____
	Yellow		____
	Red		____
	Yellow		____
	Red		____
	Yellow		____

© School District of Hillsborough County. Copying this page without written permission of Metropolitan Teaching and Learning Company is illegal.

PATTIE'S PARTY BAGS

Pattie put six toys in each of these bags.

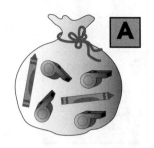

What fraction of the toys in party bag A are whistles?

What fraction of the toys in party bag B are whistles?

Which bag has the greater part that is whistles?
Circle the fraction that shows the greater part.

Pattie put 7 toys in each of these bags.

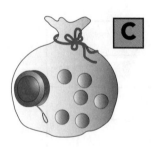

What fraction of the toys in party bag C are yo-yo's?

What fraction of the toys in party bag D are yo-yo's?

Which bag has the greater part that is yo-yo's?
Circle the fraction that shows the greater part.

216 two hundred sixteen

Name _____

BALLOONS

$$\frac{1}{4}$$

$$\frac{2}{3}$$

$$\frac{3}{4}$$

$$\frac{3}{3}$$

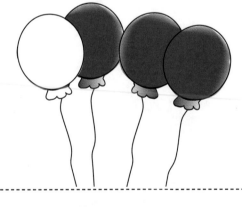

© School District of Hillsborough County. Copying this page without written permission of Metropolitan Teaching and Learning Company is illegal.

BALLOONS

$$\frac{1}{6}$$

$$\frac{5}{6}$$

$$\frac{2}{4}$$

$$\frac{1}{3}$$

© School District of Hillsborough County. Copying this page without written permission of Metropolitan Teaching and Learning Company is illegal.

TOPIC 6 Set to Party

Name _____

HOME CONNECTION: THREE OUT OF FOUR

Dear Parent or Guardian:

Your child has been learning about how fractions name part of a set. Read the instructions on the other side of this sheet aloud to your child. Then have your child complete the page.

© School District of Hillsborough County. Copying this page without written permission of Metropolitan Teaching and Learning Company is illegal.

HOME CONNECTION: THREE OUT OF FOUR

➡ Color items in each set to show the fraction.

$\frac{3}{5}$

$\frac{4}{6}$

$\frac{1}{4}$

$\frac{2}{3}$

$\frac{1}{2}$

$\frac{6}{7}$

TOPIC 6 Set to Party

TOPIC 7
Probability

© School District of Hillsborough County. Copying this page without written permission of Metropolitan Teaching and Learning Company is illegal.

Probably

HOW LIKELY IS IT?

1. It is _____ that the spinner will land on the bird than on the lion.

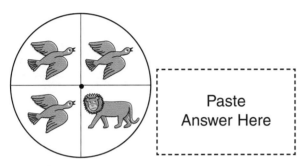

> Paste
> Answer Here

2. It is _____ that the spinner will land on the number 11.

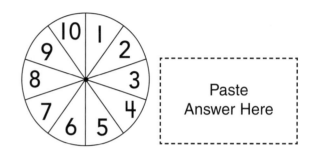

> Paste
> Answer Here

3. It is _____ that the spinner will land on a boat.

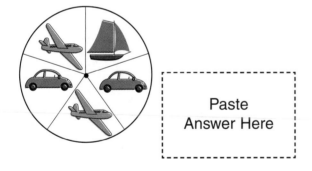

> Paste
> Answer Here

4. It is _____ that the spinner will land on a triangle or a square.

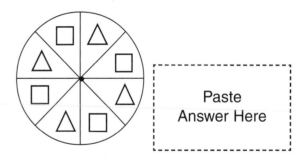

> Paste
> Answer Here

Unlikely

More Likely

Impossible

Equally Likely

Name _____

TWO-SPINNER SUMS

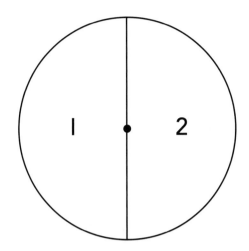

Spinner 1

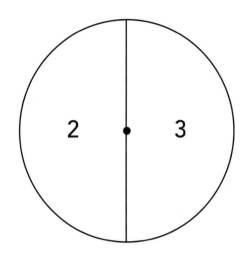

Spinner 2

Possible Outcomes		
Spinner 1	Spinner 2	Sum

Possible Sums	Number of Times Sum was Spun

1. Which sum is **most likely?** _____

2. Which sums are **equally likely?** _____

3. Name a sum that is **impossible.** _____

© School District of Hillsborough County. Copying this page without written permission of Metropolitan Teaching and Learning Company is illegal.

MORE TWO-SPINNER SUMS

➡ Write numbers in Spinner 2 that would make getting a sum of 3 <u>possible</u>.

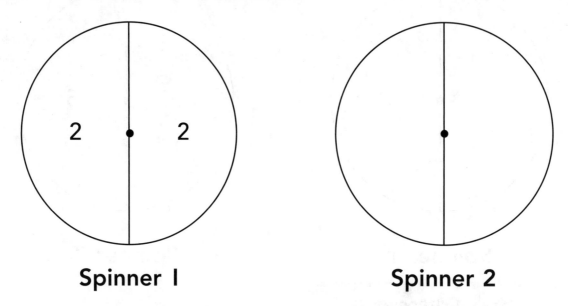

Spinner 1

Spinner 2

➡ Write numbers in Spinner 2 that would make getting a sum of 3 <u>impossible</u>.

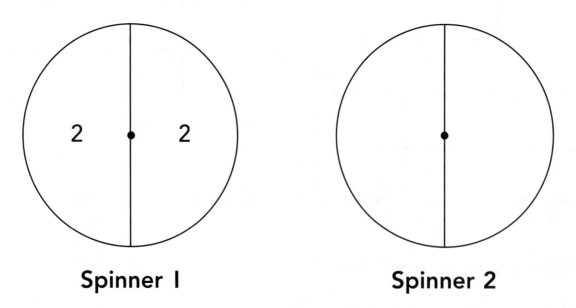

Spinner 1

Spinner 2

TOPIC 7 **Probably**

Name _____

HOME CONNECTION: MY PROBABILITY SPINNER

Dear Parent or Guardian:

Your child has been learning about probability and the likelihood of events occurring. Following the directions on the back of this sheet, your child is going to make a simple spinner to show several possible outcomes. Read the directions to your child and help him or her complete the spinner by using a paper clip and a pencil. Hold the paper clip in place at the center of the spinner with the tip of the pencil and have your child spin the paper clip.

© School District of Hillsborough County. Copying this page without written permission of Metropolitan Teaching and Learning Company is illegal.

HOME CONNECTION: MY PROBABILITY SPINNER

➡ In each section of the spinner, draw a picture of an apple, a banana, or a cherry. Draw one banana. Make the probability of landing on an apple **equally likely** to the probability of landing on a banana. Make the probability of landing on a cherry **more likely** than the probability of landing on an apple or a banana. Try at least twenty spins and record your results.

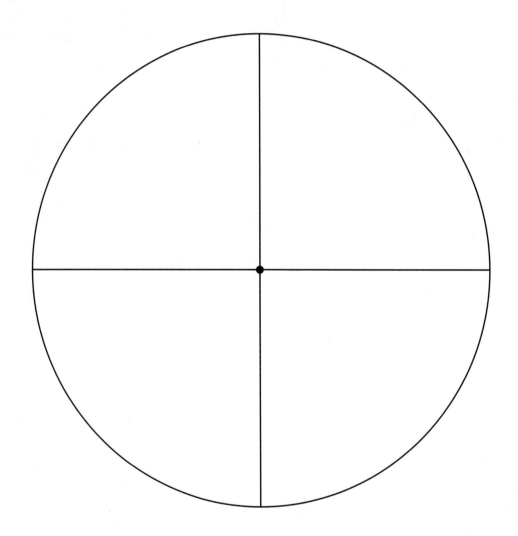

A Range of Opinion

FAVORITE FLAVORS

Ling's class voted on which flavor of ice cream they liked best—chocolate, vanilla, or strawberry. They made a tally chart of their votes.

Favorite Ice Cream

Flavor	Tally
Chocolate	⊥⊥⊥⊥ IIII
Vanilla	IIII
Strawberry	⊥⊥⊥⊥ I
Coconut	IIII

➡️ **Make a block graph to show this data. Graph the flavors in order of most popular to least popular.**

Favorite Ice Cream

What is the range of the data? _____

What is the mode of the data? _____

➡️ **Tania and Roy were late to school that day. When they came in, they voted for vanilla. The class added the votes. Fill in the new votes on the graph.**

What is the range of the new data? _____

Did the range change? _____

What is the mode of the data? _____

Did the mode change? _____

© School District of Hillsborough County. Copying this page without written permission of Metropolitan Teaching and Learning Company is illegal.

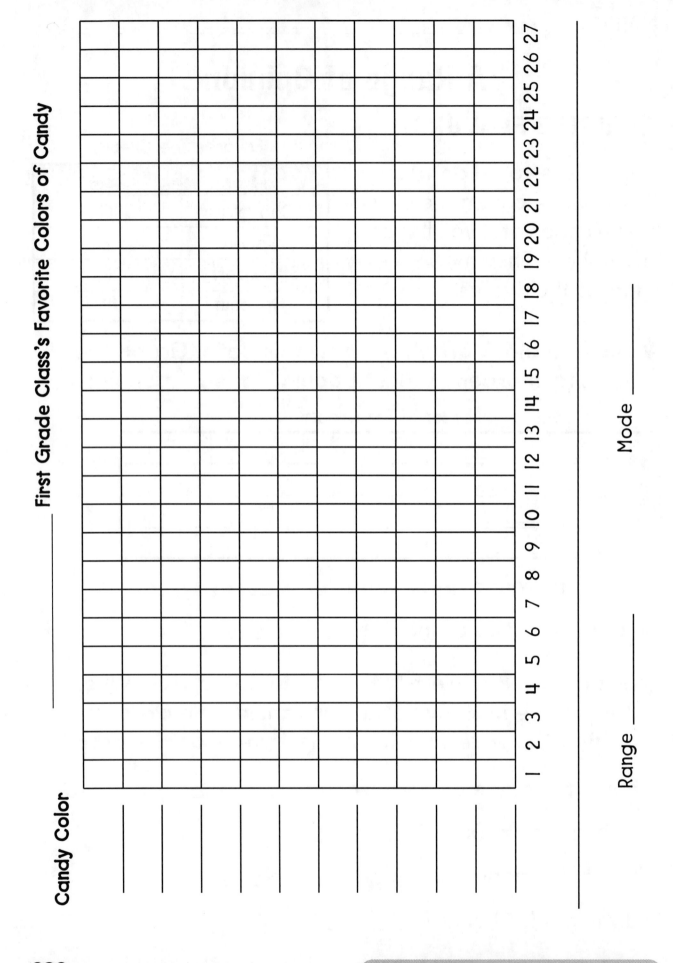

First Grade Class's Favorite Colors of Candy

Candy Color

1 2 3 4 5 6 7 8 9 10 11 12 13 14 15 16 17 18 19 20 21 22 23 24 25 26 27

Range _____

Mode _____

Name _____

HOME CONNECTION: HOW DID THEY VOTE?

Dear Parent or Guardian:

Your child has been learning about recording and analyzing data. He or she has learned that the range of a set of data is the difference between the largest and smallest value and that the mode of a set of data is the most frequently reported value. For example, suppose thirty people voted for their favorite ice cream. The results were: 10 picked chocolate, 10 picked vanilla, 6 picked strawberry, and 4 picked butter pecan. The range would be the difference between 4 and 10, or 6. The mode would be 10 because it is the number that appears most often. Read the instructions on the other side of this sheet aloud to your child. Have your child complete the page and share it with you.

© School District of Hillsborough County. Copying this page without written permission of Metropolitan Teaching and Learning Company is illegal.

HOME CONNECTION: HOW DID THEY VOTE?

➡ Use the information in the tally chart to make a block graph. Then answer the questions.

Favorite Fruit

Fruit	Tally
Apples	ЖН IIII
Oranges	ЖН IIII
Bananas	ЖН I
Pears	III

Title _____

Fruit

What is the range of the data? _____

How do you know? _____

What is the mode of the data? _____

How do you know? _____